C#.NET AND WBEMSCRIPTING

Working with Get

Richard Thomas Edwards

CONTENTS

Getting Started

THIS IS A BOOK OF CODE. It includes ASP, ASPX, HTA and HTML Reports and tables being generated by WbemScripting and Get to power them.

No book is perfect and I'm sure you will find the usual small coding issues a book of this size is naturally going to have.

Aside from that, both table and report type views are part of the source code and each of those use an assortment of controls. Below, is 99% of the pure code this book will be using. I say 99% because when the Excel Code is displayed, it uses the horizontal code for horizontal and vertical spreadsheet rendering. Also, the top up to where the enumerators start and the GetValue function will not be used in any of the coding examples. The size of this book would easily double. Instead, they are listed here and in the appendixes.

```
using System;
using System.Collections.Generic;
using System.ComponentModel;
using System.Data;
using System.Drawing;
using System.Linq;
using System.Text;
using System.Windows.Forms;
using Scripting;
using WbemScripting;

namespace WindowsFormsApplication4
{
    public partial class Form1 : Form
    {
        public Form1()
        {
            InitializeComponent();
        }
```

```csharp
private void Form1_Load(object sender, EventArgs e)
{
    SWbemLocator l = new SWbemLocator();
    SWbemServices svc = l.ConnectServer(".", "root\\cimv2");
    svc.Security_.AuthenticationLevel =
WbemAuthenticationLevelEnum.wbemAuthenticationLevelPktPrivacy;
    svc.Security_.ImpersonationLevel =
WbemImpersonationLevelEnum.wbemImpersonationLevelImpersonate;
    SWbemObject ob = svc.Get("Win32_Process");
    SWbemObjectSet objs = ob.Instances_();

    //For Horizontal Views
    foreach (SWbemObject obj in objs)
    {
        foreach (SWbemProperty prop in obj.Properties_)
        {
        }
        break;
    }
    foreach (SWbemObject obj in objs)
    {
        foreach (SWbemProperty prop in obj.Properties_)
        {
        }
        break;
    }

    foreach (SWbemObject obj in objs)
    {
        foreach (SWbemProperty prop in obj.Properties_)
        {
            foreach (SWbemObject obj1 in objs)
            {
            }
        }
        break;
    }
}
private System.String GetValue(System.String Name, SWbemObject obj)
{
    int pos = 0;
    System.String tName = Name + " = ";
    System.String tempstr = obj.GetObjectText_();
    pos = tempstr.IndexOf(tName);
    if (pos > -1)
    {
        pos = pos + tName.Length;
        tempstr = tempstr.Substring(pos, tempstr.Length - pos);
        pos = tempstr.IndexOf(";");
        tempstr = tempstr.Substring(0, pos);
```

```
        tempstr = tempstr.Replace("\"", "");
        tempstr = tempstr.Replace("{", "");
        tempstr = tempstr.Replace("}", "");
        if (obj.Properties_.Item("Caption").CIMType ==
WbemCimtypeEnum.wbemCimtypeDatetime && tempstr.Length > 14)
        {
            return tempstr.Substring(5, 2) + "/" + tempstr.Substring(7, 2) + "/" +
tempstr.Substring(0, 4) + " " + tempstr.Substring(9, 2) + ":" + tempstr.Substring(11,
2) + ":" + tempstr.Substring(13, 2);
        }
        else
        {
            return tempstr;
        }
    }
    else
    {
        return "";
    }
    }
  }
}
```

ASP Reports

Begin Code

```
    FileSystemObject fso = new FileSystemObject();

    TextStream txtstream = fso.OpenTextFile(Application.StartupPath +
"\\Win32_Process.asp", IOMode.ForWriting, true, Tristate.TristateUseDefault);

    txtstream.WriteLine("<html xmlns='http://www.w3.org/1999/xhtml'>");
    txtstream.WriteLine("<head>");
    txtstream.WriteLine("<title>Win32_Process</title>");
    txtstream.WriteLine("</head>");
    txtstream.WriteLine("<body>");
    txtstream.WriteLine("<table border='0' Cellspacing='3' cellpadding = '3'>");
    txtstream.WriteLine("<%");
```

Horizontal with no additional tags.

```
    foreach(SWbemObject obj in objs)
    {
       txtstream.WriteLine("Response.Write(\"<tr>\" + vbcrlf)");
       foreach(SWbemProperty prop in obj.Properties_)
       {
          txtstream.WriteLine("Response.Write(\"<th    align='left'    nowrap>" +
prop.Name + "</th>\" + vbcrlf)");
       }
       txtstream.WriteLine("Response.Write(\"</tr>\" + vbcrlf)");
       break;
    }
    foreach(SWbemObject obj in objs)
    {
       txtstream.WriteLine("Response.Write(\"<tr>\" + vbcrlf)");
```

```
foreach(SWbemProperty prop in obj.Properties_)
{
    txtstream.WriteLine("Response.Write(\"<td        style='font-family:Calibri,
Sans-Serif;font-size:    12px;color:navy;'    align='left'    nowrap='nowrap'>"    +
GetValue(prop.Name, obj) + "</td>\" + vbcrlf)");
}
    txtstream.WriteLine("Response.Write(\"</tr>\" + vbcrlf)");
}
```

Horizontal with a Combobox.

```
foreach(SWbemObject obj in objs)
{
    txtstream.WriteLine("Response.Write(\"<tr>\" + vbcrlf)");
    foreach(SWbemProperty prop in obj.Properties_)
    {
        txtstream.WriteLine("Response.Write(\"<th    align='left'    nowrap>"    +
prop.Name + "</th>\" + vbcrlf)");
    }
    txtstream.WriteLine("Response.Write(\"</tr>\" + vbcrlf)");
    break;
}
foreach(SWbemObject obj in objs)
{
    txtstream.WriteLine("Response.Write(\"<tr>\" + vbcrlf)");
    foreach(SWbemProperty prop in obj.Properties_)
    {
        txtstream.WriteLine("Response.Write(\"<td        style='font-family:Calibri,
Sans-Serif;font-size: 12px;color:navy;'  align='left'  nowrap='true'><select><option
value = '"  +  GetValue(prop.Name,  obj)  +  "'>"  +  GetValue(prop.Name,  obj)  +
"</option></select></td>\" + vbcrlf)");
    }
    txtstream.WriteLine("Response.Write(\"</tr>\" + vbcrlf)");
}
```

Horizontal with a link.

```
foreach(SWbemObject obj in objs)
```

```
    {
        txtstream.WriteLine("Response.Write(\"<tr>\" + vbcrlf)");
        foreach(SWbemProperty prop in obj.Properties_)
        {
            txtstream.WriteLine("Response.Write(\"<th    align='left'    nowrap>"    +
prop.Name + "</th>\" + vbcrlf)");
        }
        txtstream.WriteLine("Response.Write(\"</tr>\" + vbcrlf)");
        break;
    }
    foreach(SWbemObject obj in objs)
    {
        txtstream.WriteLine("Response.Write(\"<tr>\" + vbcrlf)");
        foreach(SWbemProperty prop in obj.Properties_)
        {

            txtstream.WriteLine("Response.Write(\"<td        style='font-family:Calibri,
Sans-Serif;font-size: 12px;color:navy;' align='left' nowrap='true'><a href='"    +
GetValue(prop.Name, obj) + "'>" + GetValue(prop.Name, obj) + "</a></td>\"    +
vbcrlf)");
        }
        txtstream.WriteLine("Response.Write(\"</tr>\" + vbcrlf)");
    }
```

Horizontal with a Listbox.

```
    foreach(SWbemObject obj in objs)
    {
        txtstream.WriteLine("Response.Write(\"<tr>\" + vbcrlf)");
        foreach(SWbemProperty prop in obj.Properties_)
        {
            txtstream.WriteLine("Response.Write(\"<th    align='left'    nowrap>"    +
prop.Name + "</th>\" + vbcrlf)");
        }
        txtstream.WriteLine("Response.Write(\"</tr>\" + vbcrlf)");
        break;
    }
    foreach(SWbemObject obj in objs)
```

```
    {
        txtstream.WriteLine("Response.Write(\"<tr>\" + vbcrlf)");
        foreach(SWbemProperty prop in obj.Properties_)
        {
            txtstream.WriteLine("Response.Write(\"<td        style='font-family:Calibri,
Sans-Serif;font-size:    12px;color:navy;'    align='left'    nowrap='true'><select
multiple><option    value    =    '"    +    GetValue(prop.Name,    obj)    +    "'>"    +
GetValue(prop.Name, obj) + "</option></select></td>\" + vbcrlf)");
        }
        txtstream.WriteLine("Response.Write(\"</tr>\" + vbcrlf)");
    }
```

Horizontal with a textarea.

```
    foreach(SWbemObject obj in objs)
    {
        txtstream.WriteLine("Response.Write(\"<tr>\" + vbcrlf)");
        foreach(SWbemProperty prop in obj.Properties_)
        {
            txtstream.WriteLine("Response.Write(\"<th    align='left'    nowrap>"    +
prop.Name + "</th>\" + vbcrlf)");
        }
        txtstream.WriteLine("Response.Write(\"</tr>\" + vbcrlf)");
        break;
    }
    foreach(SWbemObject obj in objs)
    {
        txtstream.WriteLine("Response.Write(\"<tr>\" + vbcrlf)");
        foreach(SWbemProperty prop in obj.Properties_)
        {
            txtstream.WriteLine("Response.Write(\"<td        style='font-family:Calibri,
Sans-Serif;font-size:  12px;color:navy;'  align='left'  nowrap='true'><textarea>"  +
GetValue(prop.Name, obj) + "</textarea></td>\" + vbcrlf)");
        }
        txtstream.WriteLine("Response.Write(\"</tr>\" + vbcrlf)");
    }
```

Horizontal with a textbox.

```
foreach(SWbemObject obj in objs)
{
    txtstream.WriteLine("Response.Write(\"<tr>\" + vbcrlf)");
    foreach(SWbemProperty prop in obj.Properties_)
    {
        txtstream.WriteLine("Response.Write(\"<th    align='left'    nowrap>" +
prop.Name + "</th>\" + vbcrlf)");
    }
    txtstream.WriteLine("Response.Write(\"</tr>\" + vbcrlf)");
    break;
}
foreach(SWbemObject obj in objs)
{
    txtstream.WriteLine("Response.Write(\"<tr>\" + vbcrlf)");
    foreach(SWbemProperty prop in obj.Properties_)
    {
        txtstream.WriteLine("Response.Write(\"<td    style='font-family:Calibri,
Sans-Serif;font-size: 12px;color:navy;' align='left' nowrap='true'><input type=text
value='" + GetValue(prop.Name, obj) + "'></input></td>\" + vbcrlf)");
    }
    txtstream.WriteLine("Response.Write(\"</tr>\" + vbcrlf)");
}
```

Vertical with no additional tags.

```
foreach(SWbemObject obj in objs)
{
    foreach(SWbemProperty prop in obj.Properties_)
    {
        txtstream.WriteLine("Response.Write(\"<tr><th align='left' nowrap>" +
prop.Name + "</th>\" + vbcrlf)");
        foreach(SWbemObject obj1 in objs)
        {
            txtstream.WriteLine("Response.Write(\"<td    style='font-family:Calibri,
Sans-Serif;font-size:    12px;color:navy;'    align='left'    nowrap='nowrap'>" +
GetValue(prop.Name, obj1) + "</td>\" + vbcrlf)");
```

```
        }
        txtstream.WriteLine("Response.Write(\"</tr>\" + vbcrlf)");
    }
    break;
}
```

Vertical with a Combobox.

```
foreach(SWbemObject obj in objs)
{
    foreach(SWbemProperty prop in obj.Properties_)
    {
        txtstream.WriteLine("Response.Write(\"<tr><th  align='left'  nowrap>" +
prop.Name + "</th>\" + vbcrlf)");
        foreach(SWbemObject obj1 in objs)
        {
            txtstream.WriteLine("Response.Write(\"<td   style='font-family:Calibri,
Sans-Serif;font-size: 12px;color:navy;' align='left' nowrap='true'><select><option
value = """ + GetValue(prop.Name, obj1) + """>" + GetValue(prop.Name, obj1) +
"</option></select></td>\" + vbcrlf)");
        }
        txtstream.WriteLine("Response.Write(\"</tr>\" + vbcrlf)");
    }
    break;
}
```

Vertical with a link.

```
foreach(SWbemObject obj in objs)
{
    foreach(SWbemProperty prop in obj.Properties_)
    {
        txtstream.WriteLine("Response.Write(\"<tr><th  align='left'  nowrap>" +
prop.Name + "</th>\" + vbcrlf)");
        foreach(SWbemObject obj1 in objs)
        {
```

```
            txtstream.WriteLine("Response.Write(\"<td   style='font-family:Calibri,
Sans-Serif;font-size:  12px;color:navy;'  align='left'  nowrap='true'><a  href='"  +
GetValue(prop.Name, obj1) + "'>" + GetValue(prop.Name, obj1) + "</a></td>\" +
vbcrlf)");
```

Vertical with a Listbox.

```
    foreach(SWbemObject obj in objs)
    {
        foreach(SWbemProperty prop in obj.Properties_)
        {
            txtstream.WriteLine("Response.Write(\"<tr><th align='left' nowrap>" +
prop.Name + "</th>\" + vbcrlf)");
            foreach(SWbemObject obj1 in objs)
            {

                txtstream.WriteLine("Response.Write(\"<td   style='font-family:Calibri,
Sans-Serif;font-size:    12px;color:navy;'    align='left'    nowrap='true'><select
multiple><option  value  =  "'"  +  GetValue(prop.Name,  obj1)  +  "'">"  +
GetValue(prop.Name, obj1) + "</option></select></td>\" + vbcrlf)");
            }
            txtstream.WriteLine("Response.Write(\"</tr>\" + vbcrlf)");
        }
        break;
    }
```

Vertical with a textarea.

```
    foreach(SWbemObject obj in objs)
    {
        foreach(SWbemProperty prop in obj.Properties_)
        {
            txtstream.WriteLine("Response.Write(\"<tr><th align='left' nowrap>" +
prop.Name + "</th>\" + vbcrlf)");
            foreach(SWbemObject obj1 in objs)
            {
```

```
        txtstream.WriteLine("Response.Write(\"<td    style='font-family:Calibri,
Sans-Serif;font-size:  12px;color:navy;'  align='left'  nowrap='true'><textarea>"  +
GetValue(prop.Name, obj1) + "</textarea></td>\" + vbcrlf)");
            }
            txtstream.WriteLine("Response.Write(\"</tr>\" + vbcrlf)");
        }
        break;
    }
```

Vertical with a textbox.

```
    foreach(SWbemObject obj in objs)
    {
        foreach(SWbemProperty prop in obj.Properties_)
        {
            txtstream.WriteLine("Response.Write(\"<tr><th  align='left'  nowrap>"  +
prop.Name + "</th>\" + vbcrlf)");
            foreach(SWbemObject obj1 in objs)
            {
                txtstream.WriteLine("Response.Write(\"<td    style='font-family:Calibri,
Sans-Serif;font-size: 12px;color:navy;'  align='left'  nowrap='true'><input  type=text
value="""" + GetValue(prop.Name, obj1) + """"></input></td>\" + vbcrlf)");
            }
            txtstream.WriteLine("Response.Write(\"</tr>\" + vbcrlf)");
        }
        break;
    }
```

End Code

```
    txtstream.WriteLine("%>");
    txtstream.WriteLine("</table>");
    txtstream.WriteLine("</body>");
    txtstream.WriteLine("</html>");
    txtstream.close();
```

ASP Tables

Begin Code

```
FileSystemObject fso = new FileSystemObject();

TextStream txtstream = fso.OpenTextFile(Application.StartupPath +
"\\Win32_Process.asp", IOMode.ForWriting, true, Tristate.TristateUseDefault);

txtstream.WriteLine("<html xmlns='http://www.w3.org/1999/xhtml'>");
txtstream.WriteLine("<head>");
txtstream.WriteLine("<title>Win32_Process</title>");
txtstream.WriteLine("</head>");
txtstream.WriteLine("<body>");
txtstream.WriteLine("<table border='1' Cellspacing='3' cellpadding = '3'>");
txtstream.WriteLine("<%");
```

Horizontal with no additional tags.

```
foreach(SWbemObject obj in objs)
{
    txtstream.WriteLine("Response.Write(\"<tr>\" + vbcrlf)");
    foreach(SWbemProperty prop in obj.Properties_)
    {
        txtstream.WriteLine("Response.Write(\"<th    align='left'    nowrap>" +
prop.Name + "</th>\" + vbcrlf)");
    }
    txtstream.WriteLine("Response.Write(\"</tr>\" + vbcrlf)");
    break;
}
foreach(SWbemObject obj in objs)
{
```

```
        txtstream.WriteLine("Response.Write(\"<tr>\" + vbcrlf)");
        foreach(SWbemProperty prop in obj.Properties_)
        {
            txtstream.WriteLine("Response.Write(\"<td      style='font-family:Calibri,
Sans-Serif;font-size:   12px;color:navy;'   align='left'   nowrap='nowrap'>"   +
GetValue(prop.Name, obj) + "</td>\" + vbcrlf)");
        }
        txtstream.WriteLine("Response.Write(\"</tr>\" + vbcrlf)");
    }
```

Horizontal with a Combobox.

```
    foreach(SWbemObject obj in objs)
    {
        txtstream.WriteLine("Response.Write(\"<tr>\" + vbcrlf)");
        foreach(SWbemProperty prop in obj.Properties_)
        {
            txtstream.WriteLine("Response.Write(\"<th   align='left'   nowrap>"   +
prop.Name + "</th>\" + vbcrlf)");
        }
        txtstream.WriteLine("Response.Write(\"</tr>\" + vbcrlf)");
        break;
    }
    foreach(SWbemObject obj in objs)
    {
        txtstream.WriteLine("Response.Write(\"<tr>\" + vbcrlf)");
        foreach(SWbemProperty prop in obj.Properties_)
        {
            txtstream.WriteLine("Response.Write(\"<td      style='font-family:Calibri,
Sans-Serif;font-size: 12px;color:navy;' align='left' nowrap='true'><select><option
value = '" + GetValue(prop.Name, obj) + "'>" + GetValue(prop.Name, obj) +
"</option></select></td>\" + vbcrlf)");
        }
        txtstream.WriteLine("Response.Write(\"</tr>\" + vbcrlf)");
    }
```

Horizontal with a link.

```
foreach(SWbemObject obj in objs)
{
    txtstream.WriteLine("Response.Write(\"<tr>\" + vbcrlf)");
    foreach(SWbemProperty prop in obj.Properties_)
    {
        txtstream.WriteLine("Response.Write(\"<th    align='left'   nowrap>" +
prop.Name + "</th>\" + vbcrlf)");
    }
    txtstream.WriteLine("Response.Write(\"</tr>\" + vbcrlf)");
    break;
}
foreach(SWbemObject obj in objs)
{
    txtstream.WriteLine("Response.Write(\"<tr>\" + vbcrlf)");
    foreach(SWbemProperty prop in obj.Properties_)
    {

        txtstream.WriteLine("Response.Write(\"<td      style='font-family:Calibri,
Sans-Serif;font-size: 12px;color:navy;'  align='left'  nowrap='true'><a  href='" +
GetValue(prop.Name, obj) + "'>" + GetValue(prop.Name, obj) + "</a></td>\" +
vbcrlf)");
    }
    txtstream.WriteLine("Response.Write(\"</tr>\" + vbcrlf)");
}
```

Horizontal with a Listbox.

```
foreach(SWbemObject obj in objs)
{
    txtstream.WriteLine("Response.Write(\"<tr>\" + vbcrlf)");
    foreach(SWbemProperty prop in obj.Properties_)
    {
        txtstream.WriteLine("Response.Write(\"<th    align='left'   nowrap>" +
prop.Name + "</th>\" + vbcrlf)");
    }
    txtstream.WriteLine("Response.Write(\"</tr>\" + vbcrlf)");
    break;
}
```

```
foreach(SWbemObject obj in objs)
{
    txtstream.WriteLine("Response.Write(\"<tr>\" + vbcrlf)");
    foreach(SWbemProperty prop in obj.Properties_)
    {
        txtstream.WriteLine("Response.Write(\"<td        style='font-family:Calibri,
Sans-Serif;font-size:    12px;color:navy;'    align='left'    nowrap='true'><select
multiple><option    value    =    '''    +    GetValue(prop.Name,    obj)    +    "'>"    +
GetValue(prop.Name, obj) + "</option></select></td>\" + vbcrlf)");
    }
    txtstream.WriteLine("Response.Write(\"</tr>\" + vbcrlf)");
}
```

Horizontal with a textarea.

```
foreach(SWbemObject obj in objs)
{
    txtstream.WriteLine("Response.Write(\"<tr>\" + vbcrlf)");
    foreach(SWbemProperty prop in obj.Properties_)
    {
        txtstream.WriteLine("Response.Write(\"<th    align='left'    nowrap>"    +
prop.Name + "</th>\" + vbcrlf)");
    }
    txtstream.WriteLine("Response.Write(\"</tr>\" + vbcrlf)");
    break;
}
foreach(SWbemObject obj in objs)
{
    txtstream.WriteLine("Response.Write(\"<tr>\" + vbcrlf)");
    foreach(SWbemProperty prop in obj.Properties_)
    {
        txtstream.WriteLine("Response.Write(\"<td        style='font-family:Calibri,
Sans-Serif;font-size:  12px;color:navy;'  align='left'  nowrap='true'><textarea>"  +
GetValue(prop.Name, obj) + "</textarea></td>\" + vbcrlf)");
    }
    txtstream.WriteLine("Response.Write(\"</tr>\" + vbcrlf)");
}
```

Horizontal with a textbox.

```
foreach(SWbemObject obj in objs)
{
    txtstream.WriteLine("Response.Write(\"<tr>\" + vbcrlf)");
    foreach(SWbemProperty prop in obj.Properties_)
    {
        txtstream.WriteLine("Response.Write(\"<th    align='left'    nowrap>" +
prop.Name + "</th>\" + vbcrlf)");
    }
    txtstream.WriteLine("Response.Write(\"</tr>\" + vbcrlf)");
    break;
}
foreach(SWbemObject obj in objs)
{
    txtstream.WriteLine("Response.Write(\"<tr>\" + vbcrlf)");
    foreach(SWbemProperty prop in obj.Properties_)
    {
        txtstream.WriteLine("Response.Write(\"<td      style='font-family:Calibri,
Sans-Serif;font-size: 12px;color:navy;' align='left' nowrap='true'><input type=text
value='" + GetValue(prop.Name, obj) + "'></input></td>\" + vbcrlf)");
    }
    txtstream.WriteLine("Response.Write(\"</tr>\" + vbcrlf)");
}
```

Vertical with no additional tags.

```
foreach(SWbemObject obj in objs)
{
    foreach(SWbemProperty prop in obj.Properties_)
    {
        txtstream.WriteLine("Response.Write(\"<tr><th  align='left'  nowrap>" +
prop.Name + "</th>\" + vbcrlf)");
        foreach(SWbemObject obj1 in objs)
        {
            txtstream.WriteLine("Response.Write(\"<td    style='font-family:Calibri,
Sans-Serif;font-size:    12px;color:navy;'    align='left'    nowrap='nowrap'>" +
GetValue(prop.Name, obj1) + "</td>\" + vbcrlf)");
```

```
        }
        txtstream.WriteLine("Response.Write(\"</tr>\" + vbcrlf)");
      }
      break;
    }
```

Vertical with a Combobox.

```
    foreach(SWbemObject obj in objs)
    {
      foreach(SWbemProperty prop in obj.Properties_)
      {
        txtstream.WriteLine("Response.Write(\"<tr><th align='left' nowrap>" +
prop.Name + "</th>\" + vbcrlf)");
        foreach(SWbemObject obj1 in objs)
        {
          txtstream.WriteLine("Response.Write(\"<td   style='font-family:Calibri,
Sans-Serif;font-size: 12px;color:navy;' align='left' nowrap='true'><select><option
value = """ + GetValue(prop.Name, obj1) + """>" + GetValue(prop.Name, obj1) +
"</option></select></td>\" + vbcrlf)");
        }
        txtstream.WriteLine("Response.Write(\"</tr>\" + vbcrlf)");
      }
      break;
    }
```

Vertical with a link.

```
    foreach(SWbemObject obj in objs)
    {
      foreach(SWbemProperty prop in obj.Properties_)
      {
        txtstream.WriteLine("Response.Write(\"<tr><th align='left' nowrap>" +
prop.Name + "</th>\" + vbcrlf)");
        foreach(SWbemObject obj1 in objs)
```

```
        {
            txtstream.WriteLine("Response.Write(\"<td   style='font-family:Calibri,
Sans-Serif;font-size:  12px;color:navy;'  align='left'  nowrap='true'><a  href='"  +
GetValue(prop.Name, obj1) + "'>" + GetValue(prop.Name, obj1) + "</a></td>\"  +
vbcrlf)");
```

Vertical with a Listbox.

```
    foreach(SWbemObject obj in objs)
    {
        foreach(SWbemProperty prop in obj.Properties_)
        {
            txtstream.WriteLine("Response.Write(\"<tr><th  align='left'  nowrap>"  +
prop.Name + "</th>\" + vbcrlf)");
            foreach(SWbemObject obj1 in objs)
            {

                txtstream.WriteLine("Response.Write(\"<td   style='font-family:Calibri,
Sans-Serif;font-size:    12px;color:navy;'    align='left'    nowrap='true'><select
multiple><option   value   =   "'"   +   GetValue(prop.Name,   obj1)   +   "'">"   +
GetValue(prop.Name, obj1) + "</option></select></td>\" + vbcrlf)");
            }
            txtstream.WriteLine("Response.Write(\"</tr>\" + vbcrlf)");
        }
        break;
    }
```

Vertical with a textarea.

```
    foreach(SWbemObject obj in objs)
    {
        foreach(SWbemProperty prop in obj.Properties_)
        {
            txtstream.WriteLine("Response.Write(\"<tr><th  align='left'  nowrap>"  +
prop.Name + "</th>\" + vbcrlf)");
            foreach(SWbemObject obj1 in objs)
            {
```

```
        txtstream.WriteLine("Response.Write(\"<td    style='font-family:Calibri,
Sans-Serif;font-size:  12px;color:navy;'  align='left'  nowrap='true'><textarea>"   +
GetValue(prop.Name, obj1) + "</textarea></td>\" + vbcrlf)");
            }
            txtstream.WriteLine("Response.Write(\"</tr>\" + vbcrlf)");
        }
        break;
    }
```

Vertical with a textbox.

```
    foreach(SWbemObject obj in objs)
    {
        foreach(SWbemProperty prop in obj.Properties_)
        {
            txtstream.WriteLine("Response.Write(\"<tr><th  align='left'  nowrap>"  +
prop.Name + "</th>\" + vbcrlf)");
            foreach(SWbemObject obj1 in objs)
            {
                txtstream.WriteLine("Response.Write(\"<td    style='font-family:Calibri,
Sans-Serif;font-size: 12px;color:navy;'  align='left'  nowrap='true'><input  type=text
value="""" + GetValue(prop.Name, obj1) + """"></input></td>\" + vbcrlf)");
            }
            txtstream.WriteLine("Response.Write(\"</tr>\" + vbcrlf)");
        }
        break;
    }
```

End Code

```
        txtstream.WriteLine("%>");
        txtstream.WriteLine("</table>");
        txtstream.WriteLine("</body>");
        txtstream.WriteLine("</html>");
        txtstream.close();
```

ASPX Reports

Begin Code

```
    FileSystemObject fso = new FileSystemObject();

    TextStream txtstream = fso.OpenTextFile(Application.StartupPath +
"\\Win32_Process.aspx", IOMode.ForWriting, true, Tristate.TristateUseDefault);

    txtstream.WriteLine("<!DOCTYPE html PUBLIC ""-//W3C//DTD XHTML 1.0
Transitional//EN""                  ""http://www.w3.org/TR/xhtml1/DTD/xhtml1-
transitional.dtd"">");
    txtstream.WriteLine("<html xmlns='http://www.w3.org/1999/xhtml'>");
    txtstream.WriteLine("<head>");
    txtstream.WriteLine("<title>Win32_Process</title>");
    txtstream.WriteLine("</head>");
    txtstream.WriteLine("<body>");
    txtstream.WriteLine("<table border='0' Cellspacing='3' cellpadding = '3'>");
    txtstream.WriteLine("<%");
```

Horizontal with no additional tags.

```
    foreach(SWbemObject obj in objs)
    {
      txtstream.WriteLine("Response.Write(\"<tr>\" + vbcrlf)");
      foreach(SWbemProperty prop in obj.Properties_)
      {
```

```
        txtstream.WriteLine("Response.Write(\"<th    align='left'    nowrap>"    +
prop.Name + "</th>\" + vbcrlf)");
        }
      txtstream.WriteLine("Response.Write(\"</tr>\" + vbcrlf)");
      break;
    }
    foreach(SWbemObject obj in objs)
    {
      txtstream.WriteLine("Response.Write(\"<tr>\" + vbcrlf)");
      foreach(SWbemProperty prop in obj.Properties_)
      {
        txtstream.WriteLine("Response.Write(\"<td    style='font-family:Calibri,
Sans-Serif;font-size:  12px;color:navy;'   align='left'   nowrap='nowrap'>"    +
GetValue(prop.Name, obj) + "</td>\" + vbcrlf)");
        }
      txtstream.WriteLine("Response.Write(\"</tr>\" + vbcrlf)");
    }
```

Horizontal with a Combobox.

```
  foreach(SWbemObject obj in objs)
  {
    txtstream.WriteLine("Response.Write(\"<tr>\" + vbcrlf)");
    foreach(SWbemProperty prop in obj.Properties_)
    {
      txtstream.WriteLine("Response.Write(\"<th    align='left'    nowrap>"    +
prop.Name + "</th>\" + vbcrlf)");
      }
    txtstream.WriteLine("Response.Write(\"</tr>\" + vbcrlf)");
    break;
  }
  foreach(SWbemObject obj in objs)
  {
    txtstream.WriteLine("Response.Write(\"<tr>\" + vbcrlf)");
    foreach(SWbemProperty prop in obj.Properties_)
    {
      txtstream.WriteLine("Response.Write(\"<td    style='font-family:Calibri,
Sans-Serif;font-size: 12px;color:navy;' align='left' nowrap='true'><select><option
```

```
value = '"' + GetValue(prop.Name, obj) + "'>" + GetValue(prop.Name, obj) +
"</option></select></td>\" + vbcrlf)");
        }
      txtstream.WriteLine("Response.Write(\"</tr>\" + vbcrlf)");
    }
```

Horizontal with a link.

```
    foreach(SWbemObject obj in objs)
    {
      txtstream.WriteLine("Response.Write(\"<tr>\" + vbcrlf)");
      foreach(SWbemProperty prop in obj.Properties_)
      {
        txtstream.WriteLine("Response.Write(\"<th  align='left'  nowrap>" +
prop.Name + "</th>\" + vbcrlf)");
      }
      txtstream.WriteLine("Response.Write(\"</tr>\" + vbcrlf)");
      break;
    }
    foreach(SWbemObject obj in objs)
    {
      txtstream.WriteLine("Response.Write(\"<tr>\" + vbcrlf)");
      foreach(SWbemProperty prop in obj.Properties_)
      {

        txtstream.WriteLine("Response.Write(\"<td     style='font-family:Calibri,
Sans-Serif;font-size: 12px;color:navy;'  align='left'  nowrap='true'><a  href='"  +
GetValue(prop.Name, obj) + "'>" + GetValue(prop.Name, obj) + "</a></td>\" +
vbcrlf)");
      }
      txtstream.WriteLine("Response.Write(\"</tr>\" + vbcrlf)");
    }
```

Horizontal with a Listbox.

```
    foreach(SWbemObject obj in objs)
    {
```

```
            txtstream.WriteLine("Response.Write(\"<tr>\" + vbcrlf)");
            foreach(SWbemProperty prop in obj.Properties_)
            {
                txtstream.WriteLine("Response.Write(\"<th    align='left'    nowrap>"    +
prop.Name + "</th>\" + vbcrlf)");
            }
            txtstream.WriteLine("Response.Write(\"</tr>\" + vbcrlf)");
            break;
        }
        foreach(SWbemObject obj in objs)
        {
            txtstream.WriteLine("Response.Write(\"<tr>\" + vbcrlf)");
            foreach(SWbemProperty prop in obj.Properties_)
            {
                txtstream.WriteLine("Response.Write(\"<td       style='font-family:Calibri,
Sans-Serif;font-size:    12px;color:navy;'    align='left'    nowrap='true'><select
multiple><option    value    =    '"    +    GetValue(prop.Name,    obj)    +    "'>"    +
GetValue(prop.Name, obj) + "</option></select></td>\" + vbcrlf)");
            }
            txtstream.WriteLine("Response.Write(\"</tr>\" + vbcrlf)");
        }
```

Horizontal with a textarea.

```
        foreach(SWbemObject obj in objs)
        {
            txtstream.WriteLine("Response.Write(\"<tr>\" + vbcrlf)");
            foreach(SWbemProperty prop in obj.Properties_)
            {
                txtstream.WriteLine("Response.Write(\"<th    align='left'    nowrap>"    +
prop.Name + "</th>\" + vbcrlf)");
            }
            txtstream.WriteLine("Response.Write(\"</tr>\" + vbcrlf)");
            break;
        }
        foreach(SWbemObject obj in objs)
        {
            txtstream.WriteLine("Response.Write(\"<tr>\" + vbcrlf)");
```

```
    foreach(SWbemProperty prop in obj.Properties_)
    {
        txtstream.WriteLine("Response.Write(\"<td      style='font-family:Calibri,
Sans-Serif;font-size: 12px;color:navy;' align='left' nowrap='true'><textarea>" +
GetValue(prop.Name, obj) + "</textarea></td>\" + vbcrlf)");
    }
    txtstream.WriteLine("Response.Write(\"</tr>\" + vbcrlf)");
}
```

Horizontal with a textbox.

```
foreach(SWbemObject obj in objs)
{
    txtstream.WriteLine("Response.Write(\"<tr>\" + vbcrlf)");
    foreach(SWbemProperty prop in obj.Properties_)
    {
        txtstream.WriteLine("Response.Write(\"<th    align='left'    nowrap>"    +
prop.Name + "</th>\" + vbcrlf)");
    }
    txtstream.WriteLine("Response.Write(\"</tr>\" + vbcrlf)");
    break;
}
foreach(SWbemObject obj in objs)
{
    txtstream.WriteLine("Response.Write(\"<tr>\" + vbcrlf)");
    foreach(SWbemProperty prop in obj.Properties_)
    {
        txtstream.WriteLine("Response.Write(\"<td       style='font-family:Calibri,
Sans-Serif;font-size: 12px;color:navy;' align='left' nowrap='true'><input type=text
value='" + GetValue(prop.Name, obj) + "'></input></td>\" + vbcrlf)");
    }
    txtstream.WriteLine("Response.Write(\"</tr>\" + vbcrlf)");
}
```

Vertical with no additional tags.

```
foreach(SWbemObject obj in objs)
{
```

```
    foreach(SWbemProperty prop in obj.Properties_)
    {
        txtstream.WriteLine("Response.Write(\"<tr><th align='left' nowrap>" +
prop.Name + "</th>\" + vbcrlf)");
        foreach(SWbemObject obj1 in objs)
        {
            txtstream.WriteLine("Response.Write(\"<td   style='font-family:Calibri,
Sans-Serif;font-size:  12px;color:navy;'  align='left'  nowrap='nowrap'>"  +
GetValue(prop.Name, obj1) + "</td>\" + vbcrlf)");
        }
        txtstream.WriteLine("Response.Write(\"</tr>\" + vbcrlf)");
    }
    break;
}
```

Vertical with a Combobox.

```
foreach(SWbemObject obj in objs)
{
    foreach(SWbemProperty prop in obj.Properties_)
    {
        txtstream.WriteLine("Response.Write(\"<tr><th align='left' nowrap>" +
prop.Name + "</th>\" + vbcrlf)");
        foreach(SWbemObject obj1 in objs)
        {
            txtstream.WriteLine("Response.Write(\"<td   style='font-family:Calibri,
Sans-Serif;font-size:  12px;color:navy;'  align='left'  nowrap='true'><select><option
value = '''" + GetValue(prop.Name, obj1) + "'''>" + GetValue(prop.Name, obj1) +
"</option></select></td>\" + vbcrlf)");
        }
        txtstream.WriteLine("Response.Write(\"</tr>\" + vbcrlf)");
    }
    break;
}
```

Vertical with a link.

```
foreach(SWbemObject obj in objs)
{
    foreach(SWbemProperty prop in obj.Properties_)
    {
        txtstream.WriteLine("Response.Write(\"<tr><th align='left' nowrap>" +
prop.Name + "</th>\" + vbcrlf)");
        foreach(SWbemObject obj1 in objs)
        {
            txtstream.WriteLine("Response.Write(\"<td  style='font-family:Calibri,
Sans-Serif;font-size: 12px;color:navy;' align='left' nowrap='true'><a href='" +
GetValue(prop.Name, obj1) + "'>" + GetValue(prop.Name, obj1) + "</a></td>\" +
vbcrlf)");
```

Vertical with a Listbox.

```
foreach(SWbemObject obj in objs)
{
    foreach(SWbemProperty prop in obj.Properties_)
    {
        txtstream.WriteLine("Response.Write(\"<tr><th align='left' nowrap>" +
prop.Name + "</th>\" + vbcrlf)");
        foreach(SWbemObject obj1 in objs)
        {

            txtstream.WriteLine("Response.Write(\"<td  style='font-family:Calibri,
Sans-Serif;font-size:    12px;color:navy;'    align='left'    nowrap='true'><select
multiple><option  value  =  """  +  GetValue(prop.Name,  obj1)  +  """>"  +
GetValue(prop.Name, obj1) + "</option></select></td>\" + vbcrlf)");
        }
        txtstream.WriteLine("Response.Write(\"</tr>\" + vbcrlf)");
    }
    break;
}
```

Vertical with a textarea.

```
    foreach(SWbemObject obj in objs)
    {
        foreach(SWbemProperty prop in obj.Properties_)
        {
            txtstream.WriteLine("Response.Write(\"<tr><th align='left' nowrap>" +
prop.Name + "</th>\" + vbcrlf)");
            foreach(SWbemObject obj1 in objs)
            {

                txtstream.WriteLine("Response.Write(\"<td    style='font-family:Calibri,
Sans-Serif;font-size: 12px;color:navy;' align='left' nowrap='true'><textarea>" +
GetValue(prop.Name, obj1) + "</textarea></td>\" + vbcrlf)");
            }
            txtstream.WriteLine("Response.Write(\"</tr>\" + vbcrlf)");
        }
        break;
    }
```

Vertical with a textbox.

```
    foreach(SWbemObject obj in objs)
    {
        foreach(SWbemProperty prop in obj.Properties_)
        {
            txtstream.WriteLine("Response.Write(\"<tr><th align='left' nowrap>" +
prop.Name + "</th>\" + vbcrlf)");
            foreach(SWbemObject obj1 in objs)
            {
                txtstream.WriteLine("Response.Write(\"<td    style='font-family:Calibri,
Sans-Serif;font-size: 12px;color:navy;' align='left' nowrap='true'><input type=text
value=\"\"" + GetValue(prop.Name, obj1) + "\"\"></input></td>\" + vbcrlf)");
            }
            txtstream.WriteLine("Response.Write(\"</tr>\" + vbcrlf)");
        }
        break;
    }
```

End Code

```
txtstream.WriteLine("%>");
txtstream.WriteLine("</table>");
txtstream.WriteLine("</body>");
txtstream.WriteLine("</html>");
txtstream.close();
```

ASPX Tables

Begin Code

```
FileSystemObject fso = new FileSystemObject();

    TextStream txtstream = fso.OpenTextFile(Application.StartupPath +
"\\Win32_Process.aspx", IOMode.ForWriting, true, Tristate.TristateUseDefault);

    txtstream.WriteLine("<!DOCTYPE html PUBLIC ""-//W3C//DTD XHTML 1.0
Transitional//EN""              ""http://www.w3.org/TR/xhtml1/DTD/xhtml1-
transitional.dtd"">");
    txtstream.WriteLine("<html xmlns='http://www.w3.org/1999/xhtml'>");
    txtstream.WriteLine("<head>");
    txtstream.WriteLine("<title>Win32_Process</title>");
    txtstream.WriteLine("</head>");
    txtstream.WriteLine("<body>");
    txtstream.WriteLine("<table border='1' Cellspacing='3' cellpadding = '3'>");
    txtstream.WriteLine("<%");
```

Horizontal with no additional tags.

```
    foreach(SWbemObject obj in objs)
    {
       txtstream.WriteLine("Response.Write(\"<tr>\" + vbcrlf)");
       foreach(SWbemProperty prop in obj.Properties_)
```

```
        {
            txtstream.WriteLine("Response.Write(\"<th    align='left'    nowrap>"    +
prop.Name + "</th>\" + vbcrlf)");
        }
        txtstream.WriteLine("Response.Write(\"</tr>\" + vbcrlf)");
        break;
    }
    foreach(SWbemObject obj in objs)
    {
        txtstream.WriteLine("Response.Write(\"<tr>\" + vbcrlf)");
        foreach(SWbemProperty prop in obj.Properties_)
        {
            txtstream.WriteLine("Response.Write(\"<td        style='font-family:Calibri,
Sans-Serif;font-size:    12px;color:navy;'    align='left'    nowrap='nowrap'>"    +
GetValue(prop.Name, obj) + "</td>\" + vbcrlf)");
        }
        txtstream.WriteLine("Response.Write(\"</tr>\" + vbcrlf)");
    }
```

Horizontal with a Combobox.

```
    foreach(SWbemObject obj in objs)
    {
        txtstream.WriteLine("Response.Write(\"<tr>\" + vbcrlf)");
        foreach(SWbemProperty prop in obj.Properties_)
        {
            txtstream.WriteLine("Response.Write(\"<th    align='left'    nowrap>"    +
prop.Name + "</th>\" + vbcrlf)");
        }
        txtstream.WriteLine("Response.Write(\"</tr>\" + vbcrlf)");
        break;
    }
    foreach(SWbemObject obj in objs)
    {
        txtstream.WriteLine("Response.Write(\"<tr>\" + vbcrlf)");
        foreach(SWbemProperty prop in obj.Properties_)
        {
            txtstream.WriteLine("Response.Write(\"<td        style='font-family:Calibri,
Sans-Serif;font-size:  12px;color:navy;'  align='left'  nowrap='true'><select><option
```

```
value = '" + GetValue(prop.Name, obj) + "'>" + GetValue(prop.Name, obj) +
"</option></select></td>\" + vbcrlf)");
        }
        txtstream.WriteLine("Response.Write(\"</tr>\" + vbcrlf)");
    }
```

Horizontal with a link.

```
    foreach(SWbemObject obj in objs)
    {
        txtstream.WriteLine("Response.Write(\"<tr>\" + vbcrlf)");
        foreach(SWbemProperty prop in obj.Properties_)
        {
            txtstream.WriteLine("Response.Write(\"<th    align='left'    nowrap>"    +
prop.Name + "</th>\" + vbcrlf)");
        }
        txtstream.WriteLine("Response.Write(\"</tr>\" + vbcrlf)");
        break;
    }
    foreach(SWbemObject obj in objs)
    {
        txtstream.WriteLine("Response.Write(\"<tr>\" + vbcrlf)");
        foreach(SWbemProperty prop in obj.Properties_)
        {

            txtstream.WriteLine("Response.Write(\"<td    style='font-family:Calibri,
Sans-Serif;font-size: 12px;color:navy;' align='left' nowrap='true'><a href='" +
GetValue(prop.Name, obj) + "'>" + GetValue(prop.Name, obj) + "</a></td>\" +
vbcrlf)");
        }
        txtstream.WriteLine("Response.Write(\"</tr>\" + vbcrlf)");
    }
```

Horizontal with a Listbox.

```
    foreach(SWbemObject obj in objs)
    {
```

```
        txtstream.WriteLine("Response.Write(\"<tr>\" + vbcrlf)");
        foreach(SWbemProperty prop in obj.Properties_)
        {
            txtstream.WriteLine("Response.Write(\"<th    align='left'    nowrap>"    +
prop.Name + "</th>\" + vbcrlf)");
        }
        txtstream.WriteLine("Response.Write(\"</tr>\" + vbcrlf)");
        break;
    }
    foreach(SWbemObject obj in objs)
    {
        txtstream.WriteLine("Response.Write(\"<tr>\" + vbcrlf)");
        foreach(SWbemProperty prop in obj.Properties_)
        {
            txtstream.WriteLine("Response.Write(\"<td    style='font-family:Calibri,
Sans-Serif;font-size:    12px;color:navy;'    align='left'    nowrap='true'><select
multiple><option    value    =    '"    +    GetValue(prop.Name,    obj)    +    "'>"    +
GetValue(prop.Name, obj) + "</option></select></td>\" + vbcrlf)");
        }
        txtstream.WriteLine("Response.Write(\"</tr>\" + vbcrlf)");
    }
```

Horizontal with a textarea.

```
    foreach(SWbemObject obj in objs)
    {
        txtstream.WriteLine("Response.Write(\"<tr>\" + vbcrlf)");
        foreach(SWbemProperty prop in obj.Properties_)
        {
            txtstream.WriteLine("Response.Write(\"<th    align='left'    nowrap>"    +
prop.Name + "</th>\" + vbcrlf)");
        }
        txtstream.WriteLine("Response.Write(\"</tr>\" + vbcrlf)");
        break;
    }
    foreach(SWbemObject obj in objs)
    {
        txtstream.WriteLine("Response.Write(\"<tr>\" + vbcrlf)");
```

```csharp
        foreach(SWbemProperty prop in obj.Properties_)
        {
            txtstream.WriteLine("Response.Write(\"<td        style='font-family:Calibri,
Sans-Serif;font-size:  12px;color:navy;'  align='left'  nowrap='true'><textarea>"  +
GetValue(prop.Name, obj) + "</textarea></td>\" + vbcrlf)");
        }
        txtstream.WriteLine("Response.Write(\"</tr>\" + vbcrlf)");
    }
```

Horizontal with a textbox.

```csharp
    foreach(SWbemObject obj in objs)
    {
        txtstream.WriteLine("Response.Write(\"<tr>\" + vbcrlf)");
        foreach(SWbemProperty prop in obj.Properties_)
        {
            txtstream.WriteLine("Response.Write(\"<th    align='left'    nowrap>"    +
prop.Name + "</th>\" + vbcrlf)");
        }
        txtstream.WriteLine("Response.Write(\"</tr>\" + vbcrlf)");
        break;
    }
    foreach(SWbemObject obj in objs)
    {
        txtstream.WriteLine("Response.Write(\"<tr>\" + vbcrlf)");
        foreach(SWbemProperty prop in obj.Properties_)
        {
            txtstream.WriteLine("Response.Write(\"<td        style='font-family:Calibri,
Sans-Serif;font-size: 12px;color:navy;' align='left' nowrap='true'><input type=text
value='" + GetValue(prop.Name, obj) + "'></input></td>\" + vbcrlf)");
        }
        txtstream.WriteLine("Response.Write(\"</tr>\" + vbcrlf)");
    }
```

Vertical with no additional tags.

```csharp
    foreach(SWbemObject obj in objs)
    {
```

```
        foreach(SWbemProperty prop in obj.Properties_)
        {
            txtstream.WriteLine("Response.Write(\"<tr><th align='left' nowrap>" +
prop.Name + "</th>\" + vbcrlf)");
            foreach(SWbemObject obj1 in objs)
            {
                txtstream.WriteLine("Response.Write(\"<td   style='font-family:Calibri,
Sans-Serif;font-size:   12px;color:navy;'   align='left'   nowrap='nowrap'>"   +
GetValue(prop.Name, obj1) + "</td>\" + vbcrlf)");
            }
            txtstream.WriteLine("Response.Write(\"</tr>\" + vbcrlf)");
        }
        break;
    }
```

Vertical with a Combobox.

```
    foreach(SWbemObject obj in objs)
    {
        foreach(SWbemProperty prop in obj.Properties_)
        {
            txtstream.WriteLine("Response.Write(\"<tr><th align='left' nowrap>" +
prop.Name + "</th>\" + vbcrlf)");
            foreach(SWbemObject obj1 in objs)
            {
                txtstream.WriteLine("Response.Write(\"<td   style='font-family:Calibri,
Sans-Serif;font-size: 12px;color:navy;' align='left' nowrap='true'><select><option
value = "'" + GetValue(prop.Name, obj1) + "'">" + GetValue(prop.Name, obj1) +
"</option></select></td>\" + vbcrlf)");
            }
            txtstream.WriteLine("Response.Write(\"</tr>\" + vbcrlf)");
        }
        break;
    }
```

Vertical with a link.

```
foreach(SWbemObject obj in objs)
{
    foreach(SWbemProperty prop in obj.Properties_)
    {
        txtstream.WriteLine("Response.Write(\"<tr><th  align='left'  nowrap>" +
prop.Name + "</th>\" + vbcrlf)");
        foreach(SWbemObject obj1 in objs)
        {
            txtstream.WriteLine("Response.Write(\"<td   style='font-family:Calibri,
Sans-Serif;font-size: 12px;color:navy;'  align='left'  nowrap='true'><a  href='"  +
GetValue(prop.Name, obj1) + "'>" + GetValue(prop.Name, obj1) + "</a></td>\" +
vbcrlf)");
```

Vertical with a Listbox.

```
foreach(SWbemObject obj in objs)
{
    foreach(SWbemProperty prop in obj.Properties_)
    {
        txtstream.WriteLine("Response.Write(\"<tr><th  align='left'  nowrap>" +
prop.Name + "</th>\" + vbcrlf)");
        foreach(SWbemObject obj1 in objs)
        {

            txtstream.WriteLine("Response.Write(\"<td   style='font-family:Calibri,
Sans-Serif;font-size:    12px;color:navy;'    align='left'    nowrap='true'><select
multiple><option  value  =  "'"  +  GetValue(prop.Name,  obj1)  +  "'">"  +
GetValue(prop.Name, obj1) + "</option></select></td>\" + vbcrlf)");
        }
        txtstream.WriteLine("Response.Write(\"</tr>\" + vbcrlf)");
    }
    break;
}
```

Vertical with a textarea.

```
foreach(SWbemObject obj in objs)
{
    foreach(SWbemProperty prop in obj.Properties_)
    {
        txtstream.WriteLine("Response.Write(\"<tr><th align='left' nowrap>" +
prop.Name + "</th>\" + vbcrlf)");
        foreach(SWbemObject obj1 in objs)
        {

            txtstream.WriteLine("Response.Write(\"<td   style='font-family:Calibri,
Sans-Serif;font-size:  12px;color:navy;'  align='left'  nowrap='true'><textarea>" +
GetValue(prop.Name, obj1) + "</textarea></td>\" + vbcrlf)");
        }
        txtstream.WriteLine("Response.Write(\"</tr>\" + vbcrlf)");
    }
    break;
}
```

Vertical with a textbox.

```
foreach(SWbemObject obj in objs)
{
    foreach(SWbemProperty prop in obj.Properties_)
    {
        txtstream.WriteLine("Response.Write(\"<tr><th align='left' nowrap>" +
prop.Name + "</th>\" + vbcrlf)");
        foreach(SWbemObject obj1 in objs)
        {
            txtstream.WriteLine("Response.Write(\"<td   style='font-family:Calibri,
Sans-Serif;font-size:  12px;color:navy;'  align='left'  nowrap='true'><input type=text
value='''" + GetValue(prop.Name, obj1) + "'''></input></td>\" + vbcrlf)");
        }
        txtstream.WriteLine("Response.Write(\"</tr>\" + vbcrlf)");
    }
    break;
}
```

End Code

```
txtstream.WriteLine("%>");
txtstream.WriteLine("</table>");
txtstream.WriteLine("</body>");
txtstream.WriteLine("</html>");
txtstream.close();
```

HTA Reports

Begin Code

```
FileSystemObject fso = new FileSystemObject();

TextStream txtstream = fso.OpenTextFile(Application.StartupPath +
"\\Win32_Process.hta", IOMode.ForWriting, true, Tristate.TristateUseDefault);

txtstream.WriteLine("<html xmlns='http://www.w3.org/1999/xhtml'>");
txtstream.WriteLine("<head>");
txtstream.WriteLine("<HTA:APPLICATION ");
txtstream.WriteLine("ID = ""Process"" ");
txtstream.WriteLine("APPLICATIONNAME = ""Process"" ");
txtstream.WriteLine("SCROLL = ""yes"" ");
txtstream.WriteLine("SINGLEINSTANCE = ""yes"" ");
txtstream.WriteLine("WINDOWSTATE = ""maximize"" >");
txtstream.WriteLine("</head>");
txtstream.WriteLine("<body>");
txtstream.WriteLine("<table border='0' Cellspacing='3' cellpadding = '3'>");
```

Horizontal with no additional tags.

```
foreach(SWbemObject obj in objs)
{
    txtstream.WriteLine("<tr>");
    foreach(SWbemProperty prop in obj.Properties_)
    {
        txtstream.WriteLine("<th align='left' nowrap>" + prop.Name + "</th>");
```

```
    }
    txtstream.WriteLine("</tr>");
    break;
  }
  foreach(SWbemObject obj in objs)
  {
    txtstream.WriteLine("<tr>");
    foreach(SWbemProperty prop in obj.Properties_)
    {
      txtstream.WriteLine("<td style='font-family:Calibri, Sans-Serif;font-size:
12px;color:navy;' align='left' nowrap='nowrap'>" + GetValue(prop.Name, obj) +
"</td>");
    }
    txtstream.WriteLine("</tr>");
  }
```

Horizontal with a Combobox.

```
  foreach(SWbemObject obj in objs)
  {
    txtstream.WriteLine("<tr>");
    foreach(SWbemProperty prop in obj.Properties_)
    {
      txtstream.WriteLine("<th align='left' nowrap>" + prop.Name + "</th>");
    }
    txtstream.WriteLine("</tr>");
    break;
  }
  foreach(SWbemObject obj in objs)
  {
    txtstream.WriteLine("<tr>");
    foreach(SWbemProperty prop in obj.Properties_)
    {
      txtstream.WriteLine("<td style='font-family:Calibri, Sans-Serif;font-size:
12px;color:navy;' align='left' nowrap='true'><select><option value = '" +
GetValue(prop.Name, obj) + "'>" + GetValue(prop.Name, obj) +
"</option></select></td>");
    }
    txtstream.WriteLine("</tr>");
```

```
    }
```

Horizontal with a link.

```
foreach(SWbemObject obj in objs)
{
   txtstream.WriteLine("<tr>");
   foreach(SWbemProperty prop in obj.Properties_)
   {
      txtstream.WriteLine("<th align='left' nowrap>" + prop.Name + "</th>");
   }
   txtstream.WriteLine("</tr>");
   break;
}
foreach(SWbemObject obj in objs)
{
   txtstream.WriteLine("<tr>");
   foreach(SWbemProperty prop in obj.Properties_)
   {

      txtstream.WriteLine("<td style='font-family:Calibri, Sans-Serif;font-size:
12px;color:navy;' align='left' nowrap='true'><a href='" + GetValue(prop.Name, obj)
+ "'>" + GetValue(prop.Name, obj) + "</a></td>");
   }
   txtstream.WriteLine("</tr>");
}
```

Horizontal with a Listbox.

```
foreach(SWbemObject obj in objs)
{
   txtstream.WriteLine("<tr>");
   foreach(SWbemProperty prop in obj.Properties_)
   {
      txtstream.WriteLine("<th align='left' nowrap>" + prop.Name + "</th>");
   }
   txtstream.WriteLine("</tr>");
```

```
      break;
    }
    foreach(SWbemObject obj in objs)
    {
      txtstream.WriteLine("<tr>");
      foreach(SWbemProperty prop in obj.Properties_)
      {
        txtstream.WriteLine("<td style='font-family:Calibri, Sans-Serif;font-size:
12px;color:navy;' align='left' nowrap='true'><select multiple><option value = '" +
GetValue(prop.Name,    obj)    +    "'>"    +    GetValue(prop.Name,    obj)    +
"</option></select></td>");
      }
      txtstream.WriteLine("</tr>");
    }
```

Horizontal with a textarea.

```
    foreach(SWbemObject obj in objs)
    {
      txtstream.WriteLine("<tr>");
      foreach(SWbemProperty prop in obj.Properties_)
      {
        txtstream.WriteLine("<th align='left' nowrap>" + prop.Name + "</th>");
      }
      txtstream.WriteLine("</tr>");
      break;
    }
    foreach(SWbemObject obj in objs)
    {
      txtstream.WriteLine("<tr>");
      foreach(SWbemProperty prop in obj.Properties_)
      {
        txtstream.WriteLine("<td style='font-family:Calibri, Sans-Serif;font-size:
12px;color:navy;' align='left' nowrap='true'><textarea>" + GetValue(prop.Name,
obj) + "</textarea></td>");
      }
      txtstream.WriteLine("</tr>");
    }
```

Horizontal with a textbox.

```
foreach(SWbemObject obj in objs)
{
   txtstream.WriteLine("<tr>");
   foreach(SWbemProperty prop in obj.Properties_)
   {
      txtstream.WriteLine("<th align='left' nowrap>" + prop.Name + "</th>");
   }
   txtstream.WriteLine("</tr>");
   break;
}
foreach(SWbemObject obj in objs)
{
   txtstream.WriteLine("<tr>");
   foreach(SWbemProperty prop in obj.Properties_)
   {
      txtstream.WriteLine("<td style='font-family:Calibri, Sans-Serif;font-size:
12px;color:navy;' align='left' nowrap='true'><input type=text value='" +
GetValue(prop.Name, obj) + "'></input></td>");
   }
   txtstream.WriteLine("</tr>");
}
```

Vertical with no additional tags.

```
foreach(SWbemObject obj in objs)
{
   foreach(SWbemProperty prop in obj.Properties_)
   {
      txtstream.WriteLine("<tr><th align='left' nowrap>" + prop.Name +
"</th>");
      foreach(SWbemObject obj1 in objs)
      {
         txtstream.WriteLine("<td style='font-family:Calibri, Sans-Serif;font-
size: 12px;color:navy;' align='left' nowrap='nowrap'>" + GetValue(prop.Name, obj1)
+ "</td>");
```

```
        }
        txtstream.WriteLine("</tr>");
      }
      break;
    }
```

Vertical with a Combobox.

```
    foreach(SWbemObject obj in objs)
    {
      foreach(SWbemProperty prop in obj.Properties_)
      {
        txtstream.WriteLine("<tr><th  align='left'  nowrap>"  +  prop.Name  +
"</th>");
        foreach(SWbemObject obj1 in objs)
        {
          txtstream.WriteLine("<td   style='font-family:Calibri,   Sans-Serif;font-
size: 12px;color:navy;' align='left' nowrap='true'><select><option value = '''" +
GetValue(prop.Name,   obj1)   +   '''>"   +   GetValue(prop.Name,   obj1)   +
"</option></select></td>");
        }
        txtstream.WriteLine("</tr>");
      }
      break;
    }
```

Vertical with a link.

```
    foreach(SWbemObject obj in objs)
    {
      foreach(SWbemProperty prop in obj.Properties_)
      {
        txtstream.WriteLine("<tr><th  align='left'  nowrap>"  +  prop.Name  +
"</th>");
        foreach(SWbemObject obj1 in objs)
        {
```

```
            txtstream.WriteLine("<td  style='font-family:Calibri,  Sans-Serif;font-
size: 12px;color:navy;' align='left' nowrap='true'><a href='" + GetValue(prop.Name,
obj1) + "'>" + GetValue(prop.Name, obj1) + "</a></td>");
```

Vertical with a Listbox.

```
    foreach(SWbemObject obj in objs)
    {
       foreach(SWbemProperty prop in obj.Properties_)
       {
          txtstream.WriteLine("<tr><th  align='left'  nowrap>" + prop.Name +
"</th>");
          foreach(SWbemObject obj1 in objs)
          {

             txtstream.WriteLine("<td  style='font-family:Calibri,  Sans-Serif;font-
size: 12px;color:navy;' align='left' nowrap='true'><select multiple><option value =
""" + GetValue(prop.Name, obj1) + """>" + GetValue(prop.Name, obj1) +
"</option></select></td>");
          }
          txtstream.WriteLine("</tr>");
       }
       break;
    }
```

Vertical with a textarea.

```
    foreach(SWbemObject obj in objs)
    {
       foreach(SWbemProperty prop in obj.Properties_)
       {
          txtstream.WriteLine("<tr><th  align='left'  nowrap>" + prop.Name +
"</th>");
          foreach(SWbemObject obj1 in objs)
          {

             txtstream.WriteLine("<td  style='font-family:Calibri,  Sans-Serif;font-
size:       12px;color:navy;'       align='left'       nowrap='true'><textarea>"       +
GetValue(prop.Name, obj1) + "</textarea></td>");
```

```
        }
        txtstream.WriteLine("</tr>");
    }
    break;
}
```

Vertical with a textbox.

```
foreach(SWbemObject obj in objs)
{
    foreach(SWbemProperty prop in obj.Properties_)
    {
        txtstream.WriteLine("<tr><th  align='left'  nowrap>" + prop.Name + "</th>");
        foreach(SWbemObject obj1 in objs)
        {
            txtstream.WriteLine("<td   style='font-family:Calibri,  Sans-Serif;font-size: 12px;color:navy;' align='left' nowrap='true'><input type=text value='"" + GetValue(prop.Name, obj1) + "'""></input></td>");
        }
        txtstream.WriteLine("</tr>");
    }
    break;
}
```

End Code

```
txtstream.WriteLine("</table>");
txtstream.WriteLine("</body>");
txtstream.WriteLine("</html>");
txtstream.close();
```

HTA TABLES

```
FileSystemObject fso = new FileSystemObject();

TextStream txtstream = fso.OpenTextFile(Application.StartupPath +
"\\Win32_Process.hta", IOMode.ForWriting, true, Tristate.TristateUseDefault);

txtstream.WriteLine("<html xmlns='http://www.w3.org/1999/xhtml'>");
txtstream.WriteLine("<head>");
txtstream.WriteLine("<HTA:APPLICATION ");
txtstream.WriteLine("ID = ""Process"" ");
txtstream.WriteLine("APPLICATIONNAME = ""Process"" ");
txtstream.WriteLine("SCROLL = ""yes"" ");
txtstream.WriteLine("SINGLEINSTANCE = ""yes"" ");
txtstream.WriteLine("WINDOWSTATE = ""maximize"" >");
txtstream.WriteLine("</head>");
txtstream.WriteLine("<body>");
txtstream.WriteLine("<table border='1' Cellspacing='3' cellpadding = '3'>");
```

Horizontal with no additional tags.

```
foreach(SWbemObject obj in objs)
{
    txtstream.WriteLine("<tr>");
    foreach(SWbemProperty prop in obj.Properties_)
    {
        txtstream.WriteLine("<th align='left' nowrap>" + prop.Name + "</th>");
    }
    txtstream.WriteLine("</tr>");
```

```
            break;
        }
        foreach(SWbemObject obj in objs)
        {
            txtstream.WriteLine("<tr>");
            foreach(SWbemProperty prop in obj.Properties_)
            {
                txtstream.WriteLine("<td style='font-family:Calibri, Sans-Serif;font-size:
12px;color:navy;'  align='left'  nowrap='nowrap'>" + GetValue(prop.Name, obj) +
"</td>");
            }
            txtstream.WriteLine("</tr>");
        }
```

Horizontal with a Combobox.

```
        foreach(SWbemObject obj in objs)
        {
            txtstream.WriteLine("<tr>");
            foreach(SWbemProperty prop in obj.Properties_)
            {
                txtstream.WriteLine("<th align='left' nowrap>" + prop.Name + "</th>");
            }
            txtstream.WriteLine("</tr>");
            break;
        }
        foreach(SWbemObject obj in objs)
        {
            txtstream.WriteLine("<tr>");
            foreach(SWbemProperty prop in obj.Properties_)
            {
                txtstream.WriteLine("<td style='font-family:Calibri, Sans-Serif;font-size:
12px;color:navy;'  align='left'  nowrap='true'><select><option  value  =  '"  +
GetValue(prop.Name,   obj)   +   "'>"   +   GetValue(prop.Name,   obj)   +
"</option></select></td>");
            }
            txtstream.WriteLine("</tr>");
        }
```

Horizontal with a link.

```
foreach(SWbemObject obj in objs)
{
    txtstream.WriteLine("<tr>");
    foreach(SWbemProperty prop in obj.Properties_)
    {
        txtstream.WriteLine("<th align='left' nowrap>" + prop.Name + "</th>");
    }
    txtstream.WriteLine("</tr>");
    break;
}
foreach(SWbemObject obj in objs)
{
    txtstream.WriteLine("<tr>");
    foreach(SWbemProperty prop in obj.Properties_)
    {

        txtstream.WriteLine("<td style='font-family:Calibri, Sans-Serif;font-size:
12px;color:navy;' align='left' nowrap='true'><a href='" + GetValue(prop.Name, obj)
+ "'>" + GetValue(prop.Name, obj) + "</a></td>");
    }
    txtstream.WriteLine("</tr>");
}
```

Horizontal with a Listbox.

```
foreach(SWbemObject obj in objs)
{
    txtstream.WriteLine("<tr>");
    foreach(SWbemProperty prop in obj.Properties_)
    {
        txtstream.WriteLine("<th align='left' nowrap>" + prop.Name + "</th>");
    }
    txtstream.WriteLine("</tr>");
    break;
}
```

```
foreach(SWbemObject obj in objs)
{
    txtstream.WriteLine("<tr>");
    foreach(SWbemProperty prop in obj.Properties_)
    {
        txtstream.WriteLine("<td style='font-family:Calibri, Sans-Serif;font-size:
12px;color:navy;' align='left' nowrap='true'><select multiple><option value = '" +
GetValue(prop.Name, obj) + "'>" + GetValue(prop.Name, obj) +
"</option></select></td>");
    }
    txtstream.WriteLine("</tr>");
}
```

Horizontal with a textarea.

```
foreach(SWbemObject obj in objs)
{
    txtstream.WriteLine("<tr>");
    foreach(SWbemProperty prop in obj.Properties_)
    {
        txtstream.WriteLine("<th align='left' nowrap>" + prop.Name + "</th>");
    }
    txtstream.WriteLine("</tr>");
    break;
}
foreach(SWbemObject obj in objs)
{
    txtstream.WriteLine("<tr>");
    foreach(SWbemProperty prop in obj.Properties_)
    {
        txtstream.WriteLine("<td style='font-family:Calibri, Sans-Serif;font-size:
12px;color:navy;' align='left' nowrap='true'><textarea>" + GetValue(prop.Name,
obj) + "</textarea></td>");
    }
    txtstream.WriteLine("</tr>");
}
```

Horizontal with a textbox.

```
foreach(SWbemObject obj in objs)
{
    txtstream.WriteLine("<tr>");
    foreach(SWbemProperty prop in obj.Properties_)
    {
        txtstream.WriteLine("<th align='left' nowrap>" + prop.Name + "</th>");
    }
    txtstream.WriteLine("</tr>");
    break;
}
foreach(SWbemObject obj in objs)
{
    txtstream.WriteLine("<tr>");
    foreach(SWbemProperty prop in obj.Properties_)
    {
        txtstream.WriteLine("<td style='font-family:Calibri, Sans-Serif;font-size:
12px;color:navy;' align='left' nowrap='true'><input type=text value='" +
GetValue(prop.Name, obj) + "'></input></td>");
    }
    txtstream.WriteLine("</tr>");
}
```

Vertical with no additional tags.

```
foreach(SWbemObject obj in objs)
{
    foreach(SWbemProperty prop in obj.Properties_)
    {
        txtstream.WriteLine("<tr><th align='left' nowrap>" + prop.Name +
"</th>");
        foreach(SWbemObject obj1 in objs)
        {
            txtstream.WriteLine("<td style='font-family:Calibri, Sans-Serif;font-
size: 12px;color:navy;' align='left' nowrap='nowrap'>" + GetValue(prop.Name, obj1)
+ "</td>");
        }
```

```
            txtstream.WriteLine("</tr>");
        }
        break;
    }
```

Vertical with a Combobox.

```
    foreach(SWbemObject obj in objs)
    {
        foreach(SWbemProperty prop in obj.Properties_)
        {
            txtstream.WriteLine("<tr><th  align='left'  nowrap>" + prop.Name +
"</th>");
            foreach(SWbemObject obj1 in objs)
            {
                txtstream.WriteLine("<td   style='font-family:Calibri,  Sans-Serif;font-
size: 12px;color:navy;' align='left' nowrap='true'><select><option value = ''''" +
GetValue(prop.Name,   obj1)   +   ''''>" +   GetValue(prop.Name,   obj1)   +
"</option></select></td>");
            }
            txtstream.WriteLine("</tr>");
        }
        break;
    }
```

Vertical with a link.

```
    foreach(SWbemObject obj in objs)
    {
        foreach(SWbemProperty prop in obj.Properties_)
        {
            txtstream.WriteLine("<tr><th  align='left'  nowrap>" + prop.Name +
"</th>");
            foreach(SWbemObject obj1 in objs)
            {
```

```
            txtstream.WriteLine("<td  style='font-family:Calibri,  Sans-Serif;font-
size: 12px;color:navy;' align='left' nowrap='true'><a href='" + GetValue(prop.Name,
obj1) + "'>" + GetValue(prop.Name, obj1) + "</a></td>");
```

Vertical with a Listbox.

```
    foreach(SWbemObject obj in objs)
    {
       foreach(SWbemProperty prop in obj.Properties_)
       {
           txtstream.WriteLine("<tr><th  align='left'  nowrap>" + prop.Name +
"</th>");
            foreach(SWbemObject obj1 in objs)
            {

               txtstream.WriteLine("<td  style='font-family:Calibri, Sans-Serif;font-
size: 12px;color:navy;' align='left' nowrap='true'><select multiple><option value =
"'" + GetValue(prop.Name, obj1) + "'">" + GetValue(prop.Name, obj1) +
"</option></select></td>");
            }
            txtstream.WriteLine("</tr>");
       }
       break;
    }
```

Vertical with a textarea.

```
    foreach(SWbemObject obj in objs)
    {
       foreach(SWbemProperty prop in obj.Properties_)
       {
           txtstream.WriteLine("<tr><th  align='left'  nowrap>" + prop.Name +
"</th>");
            foreach(SWbemObject obj1 in objs)
            {

               txtstream.WriteLine("<td  style='font-family:Calibri, Sans-Serif;font-
size:    12px;color:navy;'    align='left'    nowrap='true'><textarea>" +
GetValue(prop.Name, obj1) + "</textarea></td>");
```

```
        }
        txtstream.WriteLine("</tr>");
    }
    break;
}
```

Vertical with a textbox.

```
    foreach(SWbemObject obj in objs)
    {
        foreach(SWbemProperty prop in obj.Properties_)
        {
            txtstream.WriteLine("<tr><th   align='left'   nowrap>" + prop.Name +
"</th>");
            foreach(SWbemObject obj1 in objs)
            {
                txtstream.WriteLine("<td   style='font-family:Calibri,   Sans-Serif;font-
size: 12px;color:navy;' align='left' nowrap='true'><input type=text value="""" +
GetValue(prop.Name, obj1) + """"></input></td>");
            }
            txtstream.WriteLine("</tr>");
        }
        break;
    }
```

End Code

```
    txtstream.WriteLine("</table>");
    txtstream.WriteLine("</body>");
    txtstream.WriteLine("</html>");
    txtstream.close();
```

HTML Reports

Begin Code

```
FileSystemObject fso = new FileSystemObject();

TextStream txtstream = fso.OpenTextFile(Application.StartupPath +
"\\Win32_Process.html", IOMode.ForWriting, true, Tristate.TristateUseDefault);

    txtstream.WriteLine("<html xmlns='http://www.w3.org/1999/xhtml'>");
    txtstream.WriteLine("<head>");
    txtstream.WriteLine("<title>Win32_Process</title>");
    txtstream.WriteLine("</head>");
    txtstream.WriteLine("<body>");
    txtstream.WriteLine("<table border='0' Cellspacing='3' cellpadding = '3'>");
```

Horizontal with no additional tags.

```
    foreach(SWbemObject obj in objs)
    {
      txtstream.WriteLine("<tr>");
      foreach(SWbemProperty prop in obj.Properties_)
      {
        txtstream.WriteLine("<th align='left' nowrap>" + prop.Name + "</th>");
      }
      txtstream.WriteLine("</tr>");
      break;
```

```
            }
        foreach(SWbemObject obj in objs)
        {
            txtstream.WriteLine("<tr>");
            foreach(SWbemProperty prop in obj.Properties_)
            {
                txtstream.WriteLine("<td style='font-family:Calibri, Sans-Serif;font-size:
12px;color:navy;' align='left' nowrap='nowrap'>" + GetValue(prop.Name, obj) +
"</td>");
            }
            txtstream.WriteLine("</tr>");
        }
```

Horizontal with a Combobox.

```
        foreach(SWbemObject obj in objs)
        {
            txtstream.WriteLine("<tr>");
            foreach(SWbemProperty prop in obj.Properties_)
            {
                txtstream.WriteLine("<th align='left' nowrap>" + prop.Name + "</th>");
            }
            txtstream.WriteLine("</tr>");
            break;
        }
        foreach(SWbemObject obj in objs)
        {
            txtstream.WriteLine("<tr>");
            foreach(SWbemProperty prop in obj.Properties_)
            {
                txtstream.WriteLine("<td style='font-family:Calibri, Sans-Serif;font-size:
12px;color:navy;' align='left' nowrap='true'><select><option value = '" +
GetValue(prop.Name, obj) + "'>" + GetValue(prop.Name, obj) +
"</option></select></td>");
            }
            txtstream.WriteLine("</tr>");
        }
```

Horizontal with a link.

```
foreach(SWbemObject obj in objs)
{
   txtstream.WriteLine("<tr>");
   foreach(SWbemProperty prop in obj.Properties_)
   {
      txtstream.WriteLine("<th align='left' nowrap>" + prop.Name + "</th>");
   }
   txtstream.WriteLine("</tr>");
   break;
}
foreach(SWbemObject obj in objs)
{
   txtstream.WriteLine("<tr>");
   foreach(SWbemProperty prop in obj.Properties_)
   {

      txtstream.WriteLine("<td style='font-family:Calibri, Sans-Serif;font-size:
12px;color:navy;' align='left' nowrap='true'><a href='" + GetValue(prop.Name, obj)
+ "'>" + GetValue(prop.Name, obj) + "</a></td>");
   }
   txtstream.WriteLine("</tr>");
}
```

Horizontal with a Listbox.

```
foreach(SWbemObject obj in objs)
{
   txtstream.WriteLine("<tr>");
   foreach(SWbemProperty prop in obj.Properties_)
   {
      txtstream.WriteLine("<th align='left' nowrap>" + prop.Name + "</th>");
   }
   txtstream.WriteLine("</tr>");
   break;
}
```

```
foreach(SWbemObject obj in objs)
{
    txtstream.WriteLine("<tr>");
    foreach(SWbemProperty prop in obj.Properties_)
    {
        txtstream.WriteLine("<td style='font-family:Calibri, Sans-Serif;font-size:
12px;color:navy;' align='left' nowrap='true'><select multiple><option value = '" +
GetValue(prop.Name,    obj)    +    "'>"    +    GetValue(prop.Name,    obj)    +
"</option></select></td>");
    }
    txtstream.WriteLine("</tr>");
}
```

Horizontal with a textarea.

```
foreach(SWbemObject obj in objs)
{
    txtstream.WriteLine("<tr>");
    foreach(SWbemProperty prop in obj.Properties_)
    {
        txtstream.WriteLine("<th align='left' nowrap>" + prop.Name + "</th>");
    }
    txtstream.WriteLine("</tr>");
    break;
}
foreach(SWbemObject obj in objs)
{
    txtstream.WriteLine("<tr>");
    foreach(SWbemProperty prop in obj.Properties_)
    {
        txtstream.WriteLine("<td style='font-family:Calibri, Sans-Serif;font-size:
12px;color:navy;' align='left' nowrap='true'><textarea>" + GetValue(prop.Name,
obj) + "</textarea></td>");
    }
    txtstream.WriteLine("</tr>");
}
```

Horizontal with a textbox.

```
    foreach(SWbemObject obj in objs)
    {
       txtstream.WriteLine("<tr>");
       foreach(SWbemProperty prop in obj.Properties_)
       {
          txtstream.WriteLine("<th align='left' nowrap>" + prop.Name + "</th>");
       }
       txtstream.WriteLine("</tr>");
       break;
    }
    foreach(SWbemObject obj in objs)
    {
       txtstream.WriteLine("<tr>");
       foreach(SWbemProperty prop in obj.Properties_)
       {
          txtstream.WriteLine("<td style='font-family:Calibri, Sans-Serif;font-size:
12px;color:navy;' align='left' nowrap='true'><input type=text value='" +
GetValue(prop.Name, obj) + "'></input></td>");
       }
       txtstream.WriteLine("</tr>");
    }
```

Vertical with no additional tags.

```
    foreach(SWbemObject obj in objs)
    {
       foreach(SWbemProperty prop in obj.Properties_)
       {
          txtstream.WriteLine("<tr><th align='left' nowrap>" + prop.Name +
"</th>");
          foreach(SWbemObject obj1 in objs)
          {
             txtstream.WriteLine("<td style='font-family:Calibri, Sans-Serif;font-
size: 12px;color:navy;' align='left' nowrap='nowrap'>" + GetValue(prop.Name, obj1)
+ "</td>");
          }
```

```
            txtstream.WriteLine("</tr>");
        }
        break;
    }
```

Vertical with a Combobox.

```
    foreach(SWbemObject obj in objs)
    {
        foreach(SWbemProperty prop in obj.Properties_)
        {
            txtstream.WriteLine("<tr><th  align='left'  nowrap>" + prop.Name +
"</th>");
            foreach(SWbemObject obj1 in objs)
            {
                txtstream.WriteLine("<td  style='font-family:Calibri,  Sans-Serif;font-
size: 12px;color:navy;' align='left' nowrap='true'><select><option value = ''''' +
GetValue(prop.Name,   obj1)   +   '''''>"   +   GetValue(prop.Name,   obj1)   +
"</option></select></td>");
            }
            txtstream.WriteLine("</tr>");
        }
        break;
    }
```

Vertical with a link.

```
    foreach(SWbemObject obj in objs)
    {
        foreach(SWbemProperty prop in obj.Properties_)
        {
            txtstream.WriteLine("<tr><th  align='left'  nowrap>" + prop.Name +
"</th>");
            foreach(SWbemObject obj1 in objs)
            {
```

```
        txtstream.WriteLine("<td  style='font-family:Calibri,  Sans-Serif;font-
size: 12px;color:navy;' align='left' nowrap='true'><a href='" + GetValue(prop.Name,
obj1) + "'>" + GetValue(prop.Name, obj1) + "</a></td>");
```

Vertical with a Listbox.

```
    foreach(SWbemObject obj in objs)
    {
      foreach(SWbemProperty prop in obj.Properties_)
      {
        txtstream.WriteLine("<tr><th  align='left'  nowrap>" +  prop.Name  +
"</th>");
        foreach(SWbemObject obj1 in objs)
        {

          txtstream.WriteLine("<td  style='font-family:Calibri,  Sans-Serif;font-
size: 12px;color:navy;' align='left' nowrap='true'><select multiple><option value =
"'" + GetValue(prop.Name, obj1) + "'">" + GetValue(prop.Name, obj1) +
"</option></select></td>");
        }
        txtstream.WriteLine("</tr>");
      }
      break;
    }
```

Vertical with a textarea.

```
    foreach(SWbemObject obj in objs)
    {
      foreach(SWbemProperty prop in obj.Properties_)
      {
        txtstream.WriteLine("<tr><th  align='left'  nowrap>" +  prop.Name  +
"</th>");
        foreach(SWbemObject obj1 in objs)
        {

          txtstream.WriteLine("<td  style='font-family:Calibri,  Sans-Serif;font-
size:     12px;color:navy;'     align='left'     nowrap='true'><textarea>"     +
GetValue(prop.Name, obj1) + "</textarea></td>");
```

```
      }
      txtstream.WriteLine("</tr>");
    }
    break;
  }
```

Vertical with a textbox.

```
    foreach(SWbemObject obj in objs)
    {
      foreach(SWbemProperty prop in obj.Properties_)
      {
        txtstream.WriteLine("<tr><th align='left' nowrap>" + prop.Name + "</th>");
        foreach(SWbemObject obj1 in objs)
        {
          txtstream.WriteLine("<td style='font-family:Calibri, Sans-Serif;font-size: 12px;color:navy;' align='left' nowrap='true'><input type=text value='"'" + GetValue(prop.Name, obj1) + "'"'"></input></td>");
        }
        txtstream.WriteLine("</tr>");
      }
      break;
    }
```

End Code

```
    txtstream.WriteLine("</table>");
    txtstream.WriteLine("</body>");
    txtstream.WriteLine("</html>");
    txtstream.close();
```

HTML TABLES

Begin Code

```
FileSystemObject fso = new FileSystemObject();

TextStream txtstream = fso.OpenTextFile(Application.StartupPath +
"\\Win32_Process.html", IOMode.ForWriting, true, Tristate.TristateUseDefault);

    txtstream.WriteLine("<html xmlns='http://www.w3.org/1999/xhtml'>");
    txtstream.WriteLine("<head>");
    txtstream.WriteLine("<title>Win32_Process</title>");
    txtstream.WriteLine("</head>");
    txtstream.WriteLine("<body>");
    txtstream.WriteLine("<table border='1' Cellspacing='3' cellpadding = '3'>");
```

Horizontal with no additional tags.

```
foreach(SWbemObject obj in objs)
{
    txtstream.WriteLine("<tr>");
    foreach(SWbemProperty prop in obj.Properties_)
    {
        txtstream.WriteLine("<th align='left' nowrap>" + prop.Name + "</th>");
    }
    txtstream.WriteLine("</tr>");
    break;
}
```

```
foreach(SWbemObject obj in objs)
{
    txtstream.WriteLine("<tr>");
    foreach(SWbemProperty prop in obj.Properties_)
    {
        txtstream.WriteLine("<td style='font-family:Calibri, Sans-Serif;font-size:
12px;color:navy;' align='left' nowrap='nowrap'>" + GetValue(prop.Name, obj) +
"</td>");
    }
    txtstream.WriteLine("</tr>");
}
```

Horizontal with a Combobox.

```
foreach(SWbemObject obj in objs)
{
    txtstream.WriteLine("<tr>");
    foreach(SWbemProperty prop in obj.Properties_)
    {
        txtstream.WriteLine("<th align='left' nowrap>" + prop.Name + "</th>");
    }
    txtstream.WriteLine("</tr>");
    break;
}
foreach(SWbemObject obj in objs)
{
    txtstream.WriteLine("<tr>");
    foreach(SWbemProperty prop in obj.Properties_)
    {
        txtstream.WriteLine("<td style='font-family:Calibri, Sans-Serif;font-size:
12px;color:navy;' align='left' nowrap='true'><select><option value = '" +
GetValue(prop.Name, obj) + "'>" + GetValue(prop.Name, obj) +
"</option></select></td>");
    }
    txtstream.WriteLine("</tr>");
}
```

Horizontal with a link.

```
foreach(SWbemObject obj in objs)
{
   txtstream.WriteLine("<tr>");
   foreach(SWbemProperty prop in obj.Properties_)
   {
      txtstream.WriteLine("<th align='left' nowrap>" + prop.Name + "</th>");
   }
   txtstream.WriteLine("</tr>");
   break;
}
foreach(SWbemObject obj in objs)
{
   txtstream.WriteLine("<tr>");
   foreach(SWbemProperty prop in obj.Properties_)
   {

      txtstream.WriteLine("<td style='font-family:Calibri, Sans-Serif;font-size:
12px;color:navy;' align='left' nowrap='true'><a href='" + GetValue(prop.Name, obj)
+ "'>" + GetValue(prop.Name, obj) + "</a></td>");
   }
   txtstream.WriteLine("</tr>");
}
```

Horizontal with a Listbox.

```
foreach(SWbemObject obj in objs)
{
   txtstream.WriteLine("<tr>");
   foreach(SWbemProperty prop in obj.Properties_)
   {
      txtstream.WriteLine("<th align='left' nowrap>" + prop.Name + "</th>");
   }
   txtstream.WriteLine("</tr>");
   break;
}
```

```
foreach(SWbemObject obj in objs)
{
    txtstream.WriteLine("<tr>");
    foreach(SWbemProperty prop in obj.Properties_)
    {
        txtstream.WriteLine("<td style='font-family:Calibri, Sans-Serif;font-size:
12px;color:navy;' align='left' nowrap='true'><select multiple><option value = '" +
GetValue(prop.Name, obj) + "'>" + GetValue(prop.Name, obj) +
"</option></select></td>");
    }
    txtstream.WriteLine("</tr>");
}
```

Horizontal with a textarea.

```
foreach(SWbemObject obj in objs)
{
    txtstream.WriteLine("<tr>");
    foreach(SWbemProperty prop in obj.Properties_)
    {
        txtstream.WriteLine("<th align='left' nowrap>" + prop.Name + "</th>");
    }
    txtstream.WriteLine("</tr>");
    break;
}
foreach(SWbemObject obj in objs)
{
    txtstream.WriteLine("<tr>");
    foreach(SWbemProperty prop in obj.Properties_)
    {
        txtstream.WriteLine("<td style='font-family:Calibri, Sans-Serif;font-size:
12px;color:navy;' align='left' nowrap='true'><textarea>" + GetValue(prop.Name,
obj) + "</textarea></td>");
    }
    txtstream.WriteLine("</tr>");
}
```

Horizontal with a textbox.

```
    foreach(SWbemObject obj in objs)
    {
      txtstream.WriteLine("<tr>");
      foreach(SWbemProperty prop in obj.Properties_)
      {
        txtstream.WriteLine("<th align='left' nowrap>" + prop.Name + "</th>");
      }
      txtstream.WriteLine("</tr>");
      break;
    }
    foreach(SWbemObject obj in objs)
    {
      txtstream.WriteLine("<tr>");
      foreach(SWbemProperty prop in obj.Properties_)
      {
        txtstream.WriteLine("<td style='font-family:Calibri, Sans-Serif;font-size:
12px;color:navy;' align='left' nowrap='true'><input type=text value='" +
GetValue(prop.Name, obj) + "'></input></td>");
      }
      txtstream.WriteLine("</tr>");
    }
```

Vertical with no additional tags.

```
    foreach(SWbemObject obj in objs)
    {
      foreach(SWbemProperty prop in obj.Properties_)
      {
        txtstream.WriteLine("<tr><th align='left' nowrap>" + prop.Name +
"</th>");
        foreach(SWbemObject obj1 in objs)
        {
          txtstream.WriteLine("<td style='font-family:Calibri, Sans-Serif;font-
size: 12px;color:navy;' align='left' nowrap='nowrap'>" + GetValue(prop.Name, obj1)
+ "</td>");
        }
```

```
              txtstream.WriteLine("</tr>");
          }
          break;
      }
```

Vertical with a Combobox.

```
      foreach(SWbemObject obj in objs)
      {
          foreach(SWbemProperty prop in obj.Properties_)
          {
              txtstream.WriteLine("<tr><th  align='left'  nowrap>" + prop.Name +
"</th>");
              foreach(SWbemObject obj1 in objs)
              {
                  txtstream.WriteLine("<td  style='font-family:Calibri,  Sans-Serif;font-
size:  12px;color:navy;'  align='left'  nowrap='true'><select><option value = '''" +
GetValue(prop.Name,    obj1)    +    "'''>"   +    GetValue(prop.Name,   obj1)    +
"</option></select></td>");
              }
              txtstream.WriteLine("</tr>");
          }
          break;
      }
```

Vertical with a link.

```
      foreach(SWbemObject obj in objs)
      {
          foreach(SWbemProperty prop in obj.Properties_)
          {
              txtstream.WriteLine("<tr><th  align='left'  nowrap>" + prop.Name +
"</th>");
              foreach(SWbemObject obj1 in objs)
              {
```

```
            txtstream.WriteLine("<td  style='font-family:Calibri,  Sans-Serif;font-
size: 12px;color:navy;' align='left' nowrap='true'><a href='" + GetValue(prop.Name,
obj1) + "'>" + GetValue(prop.Name, obj1) + "</a></td>");
```

Vertical with a Listbox.

```
    foreach(SWbemObject obj in objs)
    {
        foreach(SWbemProperty prop in obj.Properties_)
        {
            txtstream.WriteLine("<tr><th  align='left'  nowrap>" + prop.Name +
"</th>");
            foreach(SWbemObject obj1 in objs)
            {

                txtstream.WriteLine("<td  style='font-family:Calibri,  Sans-Serif;font-
size: 12px;color:navy;' align='left' nowrap='true'><select multiple><option value =
"'"   +  GetValue(prop.Name,  obj1)  +  "'">"  +  GetValue(prop.Name,  obj1)  +
"</option></select></td>");
            }
            txtstream.WriteLine("</tr>");
        }
        break;
    }
```

Vertical with a textarea.

```
    foreach(SWbemObject obj in objs)
    {
        foreach(SWbemProperty prop in obj.Properties_)
        {
            txtstream.WriteLine("<tr><th  align='left'  nowrap>" + prop.Name +
"</th>");
            foreach(SWbemObject obj1 in objs)
            {

                txtstream.WriteLine("<td   style='font-family:Calibri,  Sans-Serif;font-
size:     12px;color:navy;'     align='left'     nowrap='true'><textarea>"     +
GetValue(prop.Name, obj1) + "</textarea></td>");
```

```
      }
      txtstream.WriteLine("</tr>");
    }
    break;
  }
```

Vertical with a textbox.

```
    foreach(SWbemObject obj in objs)
    {
      foreach(SWbemProperty prop in obj.Properties_)
      {
        txtstream.WriteLine("<tr><th   align='left'   nowrap>" + prop.Name +
"</th>");
        foreach(SWbemObject obj1 in objs)
        {
          txtstream.WriteLine("<td   style='font-family:Calibri,  Sans-Serif;font-
size: 12px;color:navy;' align='left' nowrap='true'><input type=text value="""" +
GetValue(prop.Name, obj1) + """"></input></td>");
        }
        txtstream.WriteLine("</tr>");
      }
      break;
    }
```

End Code

```
    txtstream.WriteLine("</table>");
    txtstream.WriteLine("</body>");
    txtstream.WriteLine("</html>");
    txtstream.close();
```

Initialization Code

```csharp
using System;
using System.Collections.Generic;
using System.ComponentModel;
using System.Data;
using System.Drawing;
using System.Linq;
using System.Text;
using System.Windows.Forms;
using Scripting;
using WbemScripting;

namespace WindowsFormsApplication4
{
    public partial class Form1 : Form
    {
        public Form1()
        {
            InitializeComponent();
        }
        private void Form1_Load(object sender, EventArgs e)
        {
            SWbemLocator l = new SWbemLocator();
            SWbemServices svc = l.ConnectServer(".", "root\\cimv2");
            svc.Security_.AuthenticationLevel =
WbemAuthenticationLevelEnum.wbemAuthenticationLevelPktPrivacy;
            svc.Security_.ImpersonationLevel =
WbemImpersonationLevelEnum.wbemImpersonationLevelImpersonate;
            SWbemObject ob = svc.Get("Win32_Process");
            SWbemObjectSet objs = ob.Instances_();
```

GetValue Code

```csharp
private System.String GetValue(System.String Name, SWbemObject obj)
{
    int pos = 0;
    System.String tName = Name + " = ";
    System.String tempstr = obj.GetObjectText_();
    pos = tempstr.IndexOf(tName);
    if (pos > -1)
    {
        pos = pos + tName.Length;
        tempstr = tempstr.Substring(pos, tempstr.Length - pos);
        pos = tempstr.IndexOf(";");
        tempstr = tempstr.Substring(0, pos);
        tempstr = tempstr.Replace("\"", "");
        tempstr = tempstr.Replace("{", "");
        tempstr = tempstr.Replace("}", "");
        if (obj.Properties_.Item("Caption").CIMType ==
WbemCimtypeEnum.wbemCimtypeDatetime && tempstr.Length > 14)
        {
            return tempstr.Substring(5, 2) + "/" + tempstr.Substring(7, 2) + "/" +
tempstr.Substring(0, 4) + " " + tempstr.Substring(9, 2) + ":" + tempstr.Substring(11,
2) + ":" + tempstr.Substring(13, 2);
        }
        else
        {
            return tempstr;
        }
    }
    else
    {
        return "";
    }
}
```

Stylesheets
Decorating your web pages

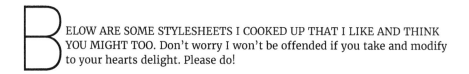

BELOW ARE SOME STYLESHEETS I COOKED UP THAT I LIKE AND THINK YOU MIGHT TOO. Don't worry I won't be offended if you take and modify to your hearts delight. Please do!

NONE

txtstream.WriteLine("<style type='text/css'>");

txtstream.WriteLine("th");

txtstream.WriteLine("{");

txtstream.WriteLine("COLOR: darkred;");

txtstream.WriteLine("BACKGROUND-COLOR: white;");

txtstream.WriteLine("FONT-FAMILY:font-family: Cambria, serif;");

```
txtstream.WriteLine("FONT-SIZE: 12px;");

txtstream.WriteLine("text-align: left;");

txtstream.WriteLine("white-Space: nowrap;");

txtstream.WriteLine("}");

txtstream.WriteLine("td");

txtstream.WriteLine("{");

txtstream.WriteLine("COLOR: navy;");

txtstream.WriteLine("BACKGROUND-COLOR: white;");

txtstream.WriteLine("FONT-FAMILY: font-family: Cambria, serif;");

txtstream.WriteLine("FONT-SIZE: 12px;");

txtstream.WriteLine("text-align: left;");

txtstream.WriteLine("white-Space: nowrap;");

txtstream.WriteLine("}");

txtstream.WriteLine("</style>");
```

BLACK AND WHITE TEXT

```
txtstream.WriteLine("<style type='text/css'>");

txtstream.WriteLine("th");

txtstream.WriteLine("{");

txtstream.WriteLine("    COLOR: white;");

txtstream.WriteLine("    BACKGROUND-COLOR: black;");

txtstream.WriteLine("    FONT-FAMILY:font-family: Cambria, serif;");

txtstream.WriteLine("    FONT-SIZE: 12px;");

txtstream.WriteLine("    text-align: left;");

txtstream.WriteLine("    white-Space: nowrap;");
```

```
txtstream.WriteLine("}");

txtstream.WriteLine("td");

txtstream.WriteLine("{");

txtstream.WriteLine("    COLOR: white;");

txtstream.WriteLine("    BACKGROUND-COLOR: black;");

txtstream.WriteLine("    FONT-FAMILY: font-family: Cambria, serif;");

txtstream.WriteLine("    FONT-SIZE: 12px;");

txtstream.WriteLine("    text-align: left;");

txtstream.WriteLine("    white-Space: nowrap;");

txtstream.WriteLine("}");

txtstream.WriteLine("div");

txtstream.WriteLine("{");

txtstream.WriteLine("    COLOR: white;");

txtstream.WriteLine("    BACKGROUND-COLOR: black;");

txtstream.WriteLine("    FONT-FAMILY: font-family: Cambria, serif;");

txtstream.WriteLine("    FONT-SIZE: 10px;");

txtstream.WriteLine("    text-align: left;");

txtstream.WriteLine("    white-Space: nowrap;");

txtstream.WriteLine("}");

txtstream.WriteLine("span");

txtstream.WriteLine("{");

txtstream.WriteLine("    COLOR: white;");

txtstream.WriteLine("    BACKGROUND-COLOR: black;");

txtstream.WriteLine("    FONT-FAMILY: font-family: Cambria, serif;");

txtstream.WriteLine("    FONT-SIZE: 10px;");

txtstream.WriteLine("    text-align: left;");

txtstream.WriteLine("    white-Space: nowrap;");
```

```
txtstream.WriteLine("    display:inline-block;");
txtstream.WriteLine("    width: 100%;");
txtstream.WriteLine("}");
txtstream.WriteLine("textarea");
txtstream.WriteLine("{");
txtstream.WriteLine("    COLOR: white;");
txtstream.WriteLine("    BACKGROUND-COLOR: black;");
txtstream.WriteLine("    FONT-FAMILY: font-family: Cambria, serif;");
txtstream.WriteLine("    FONT-SIZE: 10px;");
txtstream.WriteLine("    text-align: left;");
txtstream.WriteLine("    white-Space: nowrap;");
txtstream.WriteLine("    width: 100%;");
txtstream.WriteLine("}");
txtstream.WriteLine("select");
txtstream.WriteLine("{");
txtstream.WriteLine("    COLOR: white;");
txtstream.WriteLine("    BACKGROUND-COLOR: black;");
txtstream.WriteLine("    FONT-FAMILY: font-family: Cambria, serif;");
txtstream.WriteLine("    FONT-SIZE: 10px;");
txtstream.WriteLine("    text-align: left;");
txtstream.WriteLine("    white-Space: nowrap;");
txtstream.WriteLine("    width: 100%;");
txtstream.WriteLine("}");
txtstream.WriteLine("input");
txtstream.WriteLine("{");
txtstream.WriteLine("    COLOR: white;");
txtstream.WriteLine("    BACKGROUND-COLOR: black;");
```

```
txtstream.WriteLine("    FONT-FAMILY: font-family: Cambria, serif;");

txtstream.WriteLine("    FONT-SIZE: 12px;");

txtstream.WriteLine("    text-align: left;");

txtstream.WriteLine("    display:table-cell;");

txtstream.WriteLine("    white-Space: nowrap;");

txtstream.WriteLine("}");

txtstream.WriteLine("h1 {");

txtstream.WriteLine("color: antiquewhite;");

txtstream.WriteLine("text-shadow: 1px 1px 1px black;");

txtstream.WriteLine("padding: 3px;");

txtstream.WriteLine("text-align: center;");

txtstream.WriteLine("box-shadow: inset 2px 2px 5px rgba(0,0,0,0.5);, inset -2px -2px 5px rgba(255,255,255,0.5);;");

txtstream.WriteLine("}");

txtstream.WriteLine("</style>");
```

COLORED TEXT

```
txtstream.WriteLine("<style type='text/css'>");

txtstream.WriteLine("th");

txtstream.WriteLine("{");

txtstream.WriteLine("    COLOR: darkred;");

txtstream.WriteLine("    BACKGROUND-COLOR: #eeeeee;");

txtstream.WriteLine("    FONT-FAMILY:font-family: Cambria, serif;");

txtstream.WriteLine("    FONT-SIZE: 12px;");

txtstream.WriteLine("    text-align: left;");

txtstream.WriteLine("    white-Space: nowrap;");
```

```
txtstream.WriteLine("}");

txtstream.WriteLine("td");

txtstream.WriteLine("{");

txtstream.WriteLine("    COLOR: navy;");

txtstream.WriteLine("    BACKGROUND-COLOR: #eeeeee;");

txtstream.WriteLine("    FONT-FAMILY: font-family: Cambria, serif;");

txtstream.WriteLine("    FONT-SIZE: 12px;");

txtstream.WriteLine("    text-align: left;");

txtstream.WriteLine("    white-Space: nowrap;");

txtstream.WriteLine("}");

txtstream.WriteLine("div");

txtstream.WriteLine("{");

txtstream.WriteLine("    COLOR: white;");

txtstream.WriteLine("    BACKGROUND-COLOR: navy;");

txtstream.WriteLine("    FONT-FAMILY: font-family: Cambria, serif;");

txtstream.WriteLine("    FONT-SIZE: 10px;");

txtstream.WriteLine("    text-align: left;");

txtstream.WriteLine("    white-Space: nowrap;");

txtstream.WriteLine("}");

txtstream.WriteLine("span");

txtstream.WriteLine("{");

txtstream.WriteLine("    COLOR: white;");

txtstream.WriteLine("    BACKGROUND-COLOR: navy;");

txtstream.WriteLine("    FONT-FAMILY: font-family: Cambria, serif;");

txtstream.WriteLine("    FONT-SIZE: 10px;");

txtstream.WriteLine("    text-align: left;");

txtstream.WriteLine("    white-Space: nowrap;");
```

```
txtstream.WriteLine("    display:inline-block;");

txtstream.WriteLine("    width: 100%;");

txtstream.WriteLine("}");

txtstream.WriteLine("textarea");

txtstream.WriteLine("{");

txtstream.WriteLine("    COLOR: white;");

txtstream.WriteLine("    BACKGROUND-COLOR: navy;");

txtstream.WriteLine("    FONT-FAMILY: font-family: Cambria, serif;");

txtstream.WriteLine("    FONT-SIZE: 10px;");

txtstream.WriteLine("    text-align: left;");

txtstream.WriteLine("    white-Space: nowrap;");

txtstream.WriteLine("    width: 100%;");

txtstream.WriteLine("}");

txtstream.WriteLine("select");

txtstream.WriteLine("{");

txtstream.WriteLine("    COLOR: white;");

txtstream.WriteLine("    BACKGROUND-COLOR: navy;");

txtstream.WriteLine("    FONT-FAMILY: font-family: Cambria, serif;");

txtstream.WriteLine("    FONT-SIZE: 10px;");

txtstream.WriteLine("    text-align: left;");

txtstream.WriteLine("    white-Space: nowrap;");

txtstream.WriteLine("    width: 100%;");

txtstream.WriteLine("}");

txtstream.WriteLine("input");

txtstream.WriteLine("{");

txtstream.WriteLine("    COLOR: white;");

txtstream.WriteLine("    BACKGROUND-COLOR: navy;");
```

```
txtstream.WriteLine("    FONT-FAMILY: font-family: Cambria, serif;");

txtstream.WriteLine("    FONT-SIZE: 12px;");

txtstream.WriteLine("    text-align: left;");

txtstream.WriteLine("    display:table-cell;");

txtstream.WriteLine("    white-Space: nowrap;");

txtstream.WriteLine("}");

txtstream.WriteLine("h1 {");

txtstream.WriteLine("color: antiquewhite;");

txtstream.WriteLine("text-shadow: 1px 1px 1px black;");

txtstream.WriteLine("padding: 3px;");

txtstream.WriteLine("text-align: center;");

txtstream.WriteLine("box-shadow: inset 2px 2px 5px rgba(0,0,0,0.5);, inset -2px -
2px 5px rgba(255,255,255,0.5);;");

txtstream.WriteLine("}");

txtstream.WriteLine("</style>");
```

OSCILLATING ROW COLORS

```
txtstream.WriteLine("<style>");

txtstream.WriteLine("th");

txtstream.WriteLine("{");

txtstream.WriteLine("    COLOR: white;");

txtstream.WriteLine("    BACKGROUND-COLOR: navy;");

txtstream.WriteLine("    FONT-FAMILY:font-family: Cambria, serif;");

txtstream.WriteLine("    FONT-SIZE: 12px;");
```

```
txtstream.WriteLine("    text-align: left;");
txtstream.WriteLine("    white-Space: nowrap;");
txtstream.WriteLine("}");
txtstream.WriteLine("td");
txtstream.WriteLine("{");
txtstream.WriteLine("    COLOR: navy;");
txtstream.WriteLine("    FONT-FAMILY: font-family: Cambria, serif;");
txtstream.WriteLine("    FONT-SIZE: 12px;");
txtstream.WriteLine("    text-align: left;");
txtstream.WriteLine("    white-Space: nowrap;");
txtstream.WriteLine("}");
txtstream.WriteLine("div");
txtstream.WriteLine("{");
txtstream.WriteLine("    COLOR: navy;");
txtstream.WriteLine("    FONT-FAMILY: font-family: Cambria, serif;");
txtstream.WriteLine("    FONT-SIZE: 12px;");
txtstream.WriteLine("    text-align: left;");
txtstream.WriteLine("    white-Space: nowrap;");
txtstream.WriteLine("}");
txtstream.WriteLine("span");
txtstream.WriteLine("{");
txtstream.WriteLine("    COLOR: navy;");
txtstream.WriteLine("    FONT-FAMILY: font-family: Cambria, serif;");
txtstream.WriteLine("    FONT-SIZE: 12px;");
txtstream.WriteLine("    text-align: left;");
txtstream.WriteLine("    white-Space: nowrap;");
txtstream.WriteLine("    width: 100%;");
```

```
txtstream.WriteLine("}");
txtstream.WriteLine("textarea");
txtstream.WriteLine("{");
txtstream.WriteLine("    COLOR: navy;");
txtstream.WriteLine("    FONT-FAMILY: font-family: Cambria, serif;");
txtstream.WriteLine("    FONT-SIZE: 12px;");
txtstream.WriteLine("    text-align: left;");
txtstream.WriteLine("    white-Space: nowrap;");
txtstream.WriteLine("    display:inline-block;");
txtstream.WriteLine("    width: 100%;");
txtstream.WriteLine("}");
txtstream.WriteLine("select");
txtstream.WriteLine("{");
txtstream.WriteLine("    COLOR: navy;");
txtstream.WriteLine("    FONT-FAMILY: font-family: Cambria, serif;");
txtstream.WriteLine("    FONT-SIZE: 10px;");
txtstream.WriteLine("    text-align: left;");
txtstream.WriteLine("    white-Space: nowrap;");
txtstream.WriteLine("    display:inline-block;");
txtstream.WriteLine("    width: 100%;");
txtstream.WriteLine("}");
txtstream.WriteLine("input");
txtstream.WriteLine("{");
txtstream.WriteLine("    COLOR: navy;");
txtstream.WriteLine("    FONT-FAMILY: font-family: Cambria, serif;");
txtstream.WriteLine("    FONT-SIZE: 12px;");
txtstream.WriteLine("    text-align: left;");
```

```
txtstream.WriteLine("    display:table-cell;");

txtstream.WriteLine("    white-Space: nowrap;");

txtstream.WriteLine("}");

txtstream.WriteLine("h1 {");

txtstream.WriteLine("color: antiquewhite;");

txtstream.WriteLine("text-shadow: 1px 1px 1px black;");

txtstream.WriteLine("padding: 3px;");

txtstream.WriteLine("text-align: center;");

txtstream.WriteLine("box-shadow: inset 2px 2px 5px rgba(0,0,0,0.5);, inset -2px -
2px 5px rgba(255,255,255,0.5);;");

txtstream.WriteLine("}");

txtstream.WriteLine("tr:nth-child(even);{background-color:#f2f2f2;}");

txtstream.WriteLine("tr:nth-child(odd);{background-color:#cccccc;
color:#f2f2f2;}");

txtstream.WriteLine("</style>");
```

GHOST DECORATED

```
txtstream.WriteLine("<style type='text/css'>");

txtstream.WriteLine("th");

txtstream.WriteLine("{");

txtstream.WriteLine("    COLOR: black;");

txtstream.WriteLine("    BACKGROUND-COLOR: white;");

txtstream.WriteLine("    FONT-FAMILY:font-family: Cambria, serif;");

txtstream.WriteLine("    FONT-SIZE: 12px;");

txtstream.WriteLine("    text-align: left;");

txtstream.WriteLine("    white-Space: nowrap;");

txtstream.WriteLine("}");
```

```
txtstream.WriteLine("td");
txtstream.WriteLine("{");
txtstream.WriteLine("    COLOR: black;");
txtstream.WriteLine("    BACKGROUND-COLOR: white;");
txtstream.WriteLine("    FONT-FAMILY: font-family: Cambria, serif;");
txtstream.WriteLine("    FONT-SIZE: 12px;");
txtstream.WriteLine("    text-align: left;");
txtstream.WriteLine("    white-Space: nowrap;");
txtstream.WriteLine("}");
txtstream.WriteLine("div");
txtstream.WriteLine("{");
txtstream.WriteLine("    COLOR: black;");
txtstream.WriteLine("    BACKGROUND-COLOR: white;");
txtstream.WriteLine("    FONT-FAMILY: font-family: Cambria, serif;");
txtstream.WriteLine("    FONT-SIZE: 10px;");
txtstream.WriteLine("    text-align: left;");
txtstream.WriteLine("    white-Space: nowrap;");
txtstream.WriteLine("}");
txtstream.WriteLine("span");
txtstream.WriteLine("{");
txtstream.WriteLine("    COLOR: black;");
txtstream.WriteLine("    BACKGROUND-COLOR: white;");
txtstream.WriteLine("    FONT-FAMILY: font-family: Cambria, serif;");
txtstream.WriteLine("    FONT-SIZE: 10px;");
txtstream.WriteLine("    text-align: left;");
txtstream.WriteLine("    white-Space: nowrap;");
txtstream.WriteLine("    display:inline-block;");
```

```
txtstream.WriteLine("    width: 100%;");
txtstream.WriteLine("}");
txtstream.WriteLine("textarea");
txtstream.WriteLine("{");
txtstream.WriteLine("    COLOR: black;");
txtstream.WriteLine("    BACKGROUND-COLOR: white;");
txtstream.WriteLine("    FONT-FAMILY: font-family: Cambria, serif;");
txtstream.WriteLine("    FONT-SIZE: 10px;");
txtstream.WriteLine("    text-align: left;");
txtstream.WriteLine("    white-Space: nowrap;");
txtstream.WriteLine("    width: 100%;");
txtstream.WriteLine("}");
txtstream.WriteLine("select");
txtstream.WriteLine("{");
txtstream.WriteLine("    COLOR: black;");
txtstream.WriteLine("    BACKGROUND-COLOR: white;");
txtstream.WriteLine("    FONT-FAMILY: font-family: Cambria, serif;");
txtstream.WriteLine("    FONT-SIZE: 10px;");
txtstream.WriteLine("    text-align: left;");
txtstream.WriteLine("    white-Space: nowrap;");
txtstream.WriteLine("    width: 100%;");
txtstream.WriteLine("}");
txtstream.WriteLine("input");
txtstream.WriteLine("{");
txtstream.WriteLine("    COLOR: black;");
txtstream.WriteLine("    BACKGROUND-COLOR: white;");
txtstream.WriteLine("    FONT-FAMILY: font-family: Cambria, serif;");
```

```
txtstream.WriteLine("   FONT-SIZE: 12px;");

txtstream.WriteLine("   text-align: left;");

txtstream.WriteLine("   display:table-cell;");

txtstream.WriteLine("   white-Space: nowrap;");

txtstream.WriteLine("}");

txtstream.WriteLine("h1 {");

txtstream.WriteLine("color: antiquewhite;");

txtstream.WriteLine("text-shadow: 1px 1px 1px black;");

txtstream.WriteLine("padding: 3px;");

txtstream.WriteLine("text-align: center;");

txtstream.WriteLine("box-shadow: inset 2px 2px 5px rgba(0,0,0,0.5);, inset -2px -2px 5px rgba(255,255,255,0.5);;");

txtstream.WriteLine("}");

txtstream.WriteLine("</style>");
```

3D

```
txtstream.WriteLine("<style type='text/css'>");

txtstream.WriteLine("body");

txtstream.WriteLine("{");

txtstream.WriteLine("   PADDING-RIGHT: 0px;");

txtstream.WriteLine("   PADDING-LEFT: 0px;");

txtstream.WriteLine("   PADDING-BOTTOM: 0px;");

txtstream.WriteLine("   MARGIN: 0px;");

txtstream.WriteLine("   COLOR: #333;");

txtstream.WriteLine("   PADDING-TOP: 0px;");
```

```
txtstream.WriteLine("    FONT-FAMILY: verdana, arial, helvetica, sans-serif;");
txtstream.WriteLine("}");
txtstream.WriteLine("table");
txtstream.WriteLine("{");
txtstream.WriteLine("    BORDER-RIGHT: #999999 3px solid;");
txtstream.WriteLine("    PADDING-RIGHT: 6px;");
txtstream.WriteLine("    PADDING-LEFT: 6px;");
txtstream.WriteLine("    FONT-WEIGHT: Bold;");
txtstream.WriteLine("    FONT-SIZE: 14px;");
txtstream.WriteLine("    PADDING-BOTTOM: 6px;");
txtstream.WriteLine("    COLOR: Peru;");
txtstream.WriteLine("    LINE-HEIGHT: 14px;");
txtstream.WriteLine("    PADDING-TOP: 6px;");
txtstream.WriteLine("    BORDER-BOTTOM: #999 1px solid;");
txtstream.WriteLine("    BACKGROUND-COLOR: #eeeeee;");
txtstream.WriteLine("    FONT-FAMILY: verdana, arial, helvetica, sans-serif;");
txtstream.WriteLine("    FONT-SIZE: 12px;");
txtstream.WriteLine("}");
txtstream.WriteLine("th");
txtstream.WriteLine("{");
txtstream.WriteLine("    BORDER-RIGHT: #999999 3px solid;");
txtstream.WriteLine("    PADDING-RIGHT: 6px;");
txtstream.WriteLine("    PADDING-LEFT: 6px;");
txtstream.WriteLine("    FONT-WEIGHT: Bold;");
txtstream.WriteLine("    FONT-SIZE: 14px;");
txtstream.WriteLine("    PADDING-BOTTOM: 6px;");
txtstream.WriteLine("    COLOR: darkred;");
```

```
txtstream.WriteLine("    LINE-HEIGHT: 14px;");
txtstream.WriteLine("    PADDING-TOP: 6px;");
txtstream.WriteLine("    BORDER-BOTTOM: #999 1px solid;");
txtstream.WriteLine("    BACKGROUND-COLOR: #eeeeee;");
txtstream.WriteLine("    FONT-FAMILY:font-family: Cambria, serif;");
txtstream.WriteLine("    FONT-SIZE: 12px;");
txtstream.WriteLine("    text-align: left;");
txtstream.WriteLine("    white-Space: nowrap;");
txtstream.WriteLine("}");
txtstream.WriteLine(".th");
txtstream.WriteLine("{");
txtstream.WriteLine("    BORDER-RIGHT: #999999 2px solid;");
txtstream.WriteLine("    PADDING-RIGHT: 6px;");
txtstream.WriteLine("    PADDING-LEFT: 6px;");
txtstream.WriteLine("    FONT-WEIGHT: Bold;");
txtstrcam.WriteLine("    PADDING-BOTTOM: 6px;");
txtstream.WriteLine("    COLOR: black;");
txtstream.WriteLine("    PADDING-TOP: 6px;");
txtstream.WriteLine("    BORDER-BOTTOM: #999 2px solid;");
txtstream.WriteLine("    BACKGROUND-COLOR: #eeeeee;");
txtstream.WriteLine("    FONT-FAMILY: font-family: Cambria, serif;");
txtstream.WriteLine("    FONT-SIZE: 10px;");
txtstream.WriteLine("    text-align: right;");
txtstream.WriteLine("    white-Space: nowrap;");
txtstream.WriteLine("}");
txtstream.WriteLine("td");
txtstream.WriteLine("{");
```

```
txtstream.WriteLine("    BORDER-RIGHT: #999999 3px solid;");

txtstream.WriteLine("    PADDING-RIGHT: 6px;");

txtstream.WriteLine("    PADDING-LEFT: 6px;");

txtstream.WriteLine("    FONT-WEIGHT: Normal;");

txtstream.WriteLine("    PADDING-BOTTOM: 6px;");

txtstream.WriteLine("    COLOR: navy;");

txtstream.WriteLine("    LINE-HEIGHT: 14px;");

txtstream.WriteLine("    PADDING-TOP: 6px;");

txtstream.WriteLine("    BORDER-BOTTOM: #999 1px solid;");

txtstream.WriteLine("    BACKGROUND-COLOR: #eeeeee;");

txtstream.WriteLine("    FONT-FAMILY: font-family: Cambria, serif;");

txtstream.WriteLine("    FONT-SIZE: 12px;");

txtstream.WriteLine("    text-align: left;");

txtstream.WriteLine("    white-Space: nowrap;");

txtstream.WriteLine("}");

txtstream.WriteLine("div");

txtstream.WriteLine("{");

txtstream.WriteLine("    BORDER-RIGHT: #999999 3px solid;");

txtstream.WriteLine("    PADDING-RIGHT: 6px;");

txtstream.WriteLine("    PADDING-LEFT: 6px;");

txtstream.WriteLine("    FONT-WEIGHT: Normal;");

txtstream.WriteLine("    PADDING-BOTTOM: 6px;");

txtstream.WriteLine("    COLOR: white;");

txtstream.WriteLine("    PADDING-TOP: 6px;");

txtstream.WriteLine("    BORDER-BOTTOM: #999 1px solid;");

txtstream.WriteLine("    BACKGROUND-COLOR: navy;");

txtstream.WriteLine("    FONT-FAMILY: font-family: Cambria, serif;");
```

```
txtstream.WriteLine("    FONT-SIZE: 10px;");
txtstream.WriteLine("    text-align: left;");
txtstream.WriteLine("    white-Space: nowrap;");
txtstream.WriteLine("}");
txtstream.WriteLine("span");
txtstream.WriteLine("{");
txtstream.WriteLine("    BORDER-RIGHT: #999999 3px solid;");
txtstream.WriteLine("    PADDING-RIGHT: 3px;");
txtstream.WriteLine("    PADDING-LEFT: 3px;");
txtstream.WriteLine("    FONT-WEIGHT: Normal;");
txtstream.WriteLine("    PADDING-BOTTOM: 3px;");
txtstream.WriteLine("    COLOR: white;");
txtstream.WriteLine("    PADDING-TOP: 3px;");
txtstream.WriteLine("    BORDER-BOTTOM: #999 1px solid;");
txtstream.WriteLine("    BACKGROUND-COLOR: navy;");
txtstream.WriteLine("    FONT-FAMILY: font-family: Cambria, serif;");
txtstream.WriteLine("    FONT-SIZE: 10px;");
txtstream.WriteLine("    text-align: left;");
txtstream.WriteLine("    white-Space: nowrap;");
txtstream.WriteLine("    display:inline-block;");
txtstream.WriteLine("    width: 100%;");
txtstream.WriteLine("}");
txtstream.WriteLine("textarea");
txtstream.WriteLine("{");
txtstream.WriteLine("    BORDER-RIGHT: #999999 3px solid;");
txtstream.WriteLine("    PADDING-RIGHT: 3px;");
txtstream.WriteLine("    PADDING-LEFT: 3px;");
```

```
txtstream.WriteLine("    FONT-WEIGHT: Normal;");
txtstream.WriteLine("    PADDING-BOTTOM: 3px;");
txtstream.WriteLine("    COLOR: white;");
txtstream.WriteLine("    PADDING-TOP: 3px;");
txtstream.WriteLine("    BORDER-BOTTOM: #999 1px solid;");
txtstream.WriteLine("    BACKGROUND-COLOR: navy;");
txtstream.WriteLine("    FONT-FAMILY: font-family: Cambria, serif;");
txtstream.WriteLine("    FONT-SIZE: 10px;");
txtstream.WriteLine("    text-align: left;");
txtstream.WriteLine("    white-Space: nowrap;");
txtstream.WriteLine("    width: 100%;");
txtstream.WriteLine("}");
txtstream.WriteLine("select");
txtstream.WriteLine("{");
txtstream.WriteLine("    BORDER-RIGHT: #999999 3px solid;");
txtstream.WriteLine("    PADDING-RIGHT: 6px;");
txtstream.WriteLine("    PADDING-LEFT: 6px;");
txtstream.WriteLine("    FONT-WEIGHT: Normal;");
txtstream.WriteLine("    PADDING-BOTTOM: 6px;");
txtstream.WriteLine("    COLOR: white;");
txtstream.WriteLine("    PADDING-TOP: 6px;");
txtstream.WriteLine("    BORDER-BOTTOM: #999 1px solid;");
txtstream.WriteLine("    BACKGROUND-COLOR: navy;");
txtstream.WriteLine("    FONT-FAMILY: font-family: Cambria, serif;");
txtstream.WriteLine("    FONT-SIZE: 10px;");
txtstream.WriteLine("    text-align: left;");
txtstream.WriteLine("    white-Space: nowrap;");
```

```
txtstream.WriteLine("    width: 100%;");

txtstream.WriteLine("}");

txtstream.WriteLine("input");

txtstream.WriteLine("{");

txtstream.WriteLine("    BORDER-RIGHT: #999999 3px solid;");

txtstream.WriteLine("    PADDING-RIGHT: 3px;");

txtstream.WriteLine("    PADDING-LEFT: 3px;");

txtstream.WriteLine("    FONT-WEIGHT: Bold;");

txtstream.WriteLine("    PADDING-BOTTOM: 3px;");

txtstream.WriteLine("    COLOR: white;");

txtstream.WriteLine("    PADDING-TOP: 3px;");

txtstream.WriteLine("    BORDER-BOTTOM: #999 1px solid;");

txtstream.WriteLine("    BACKGROUND-COLOR: navy;");

txtstream.WriteLine("    FONT-FAMILY: font-family: Cambria, serif;");

txtstream.WriteLine("    FONT-SIZE: 12px;");

txtstream.WriteLine("    text-align: left;");

txtstream.WriteLine("    display:table-cell;");

txtstream.WriteLine("    white-Space: nowrap;");

txtstream.WriteLine("    width: 100%;");

txtstream.WriteLine("}");

txtstream.WriteLine("h1 {");

txtstream.WriteLine("color: antiquewhite;");

txtstream.WriteLine("text-shadow: 1px 1px 1px black;");

txtstream.WriteLine("padding: 3px;");

txtstream.WriteLine("text-align: center;");

txtstream.WriteLine("box-shadow: inset 2px 2px 5px rgba(0,0,0,0.5);, inset -2px -2px 5px rgba(255,255,255,0.5);;");
```

txtstream.WriteLine("}");

txtstream.WriteLine("</style>");

SHADOW BOX

txtstream.WriteLine("<style type='text/css'>");

txtstream.WriteLine("body");

txtstream.WriteLine("{");

txtstream.WriteLine("   PADDING-RIGHT: 0px;");

txtstream.WriteLine("   PADDING-LEFT: 0px;");

txtstream.WriteLine("   PADDING-BOTTOM: 0px;");

txtstream.WriteLine("   MARGIN: 0px;");

txtstream.WriteLine("   COLOR: #333;");

txtstream.WriteLine("   PADDING-TOP: 0px;");

txtstream.WriteLine("   FONT-FAMILY: verdana, arial, helvetica, sans-serif;");

txtstream.WriteLine("}");

txtstream.WriteLine("table");

txtstream.WriteLine("{");

txtstream.WriteLine("   BORDER-RIGHT: #999999 1px solid;");

txtstream.WriteLine("   PADDING-RIGHT: 1px;");

txtstream.WriteLine("   PADDING-LEFT: 1px;");

txtstream.WriteLine("   PADDING-BOTTOM: 1px;");

txtstream.WriteLine("   LINE-HEIGHT: 8px;");

txtstream.WriteLine("   PADDING-TOP: 1px;");

txtstream.WriteLine("   BORDER-BOTTOM: #999 1px solid;");

txtstream.WriteLine("   BACKGROUND-COLOR: #eeeeee;");

```
txtstream.WriteLine("
filter:progid:DXImageTransform.Microsoft.Shadow(color='silver', Direction=135,
Strength=16");

txtstream.WriteLine("}");

txtstream.WriteLine("th");

txtstream.WriteLine("{");

txtstream.WriteLine("    BORDER-RIGHT: #999999 3px solid;");

txtstream.WriteLine("    PADDING-RIGHT: 6px;");

txtstream.WriteLine("    PADDING-LEFT: 6px;");

txtstream.WriteLine("    FONT-WEIGHT: Bold;");

txtstream.WriteLine("    FONT-SIZE: 14px;");

txtstream.WriteLine("    PADDING-BOTTOM: 6px;");

txtstream.WriteLine("    COLOR: darkred;");

txtstream.WriteLine("    LINE-HEIGHT: 14px;");

txtstream.WriteLine("    PADDING-TOP: 6px;");

txtstream.WriteLine("    BORDER-BOTTOM: #999 1px solid;");

txtstream.WriteLine("    BACKGROUND-COLOR: #eeeeee;");

txtstream.WriteLine("    FONT-FAMILY: font-family: Cambria, serif;");

txtstream.WriteLine("    FONT-SIZE: 12px;");

txtstream.WriteLine("    text-align: left;");

txtstream.WriteLine("    white-Space: nowrap;");

txtstream.WriteLine("}");

txtstream.WriteLine(".th");

txtstream.WriteLine("{");

txtstream.WriteLine("    BORDER-RIGHT: #999999 2px solid;");

txtstream.WriteLine("    PADDING-RIGHT: 6px;");

txtstream.WriteLine("    PADDING-LEFT: 6px;");

txtstream.WriteLine("    FONT-WEIGHT: Bold;");
```

```
txtstream.WriteLine("    PADDING-BOTTOM: 6px;");
txtstream.WriteLine("    COLOR: black;");
txtstream.WriteLine("    PADDING-TOP: 6px;");
txtstream.WriteLine("    BORDER-BOTTOM: #999 2px solid;");
txtstream.WriteLine("    BACKGROUND-COLOR: #eeeeee;");
txtstream.WriteLine("    FONT-FAMILY: font-family: Cambria, serif;");
txtstream.WriteLine("    FONT-SIZE: 10px;");
txtstream.WriteLine("    text-align: right;");
txtstream.WriteLine("    white-Space: nowrap;");
txtstream.WriteLine("}");
txtstream.WriteLine("td");
txtstream.WriteLine("{");
txtstream.WriteLine("    BORDER-RIGHT: #999999 3px solid;");
txtstream.WriteLine("    PADDING-RIGHT: 6px;");
txtstream.WriteLine("    PADDING-LEFT: 6px;");
txtstream.WriteLine("    FONT-WEIGHT: Normal;");
txtstream.WriteLine("    PADDING-BOTTOM: 6px;");
txtstream.WriteLine("    COLOR: navy;");
txtstream.WriteLine("    LINE-HEIGHT: 14px;");
txtstream.WriteLine("    PADDING-TOP: 6px;");
txtstream.WriteLine("    BORDER-BOTTOM: #999 1px solid;");
txtstream.WriteLine("    BACKGROUND-COLOR: #eeeeee;");
txtstream.WriteLine("    FONT-FAMILY: font-family: Cambria, serif;");
txtstream.WriteLine("    FONT-SIZE: 12px;");
txtstream.WriteLine("    text-align: left;");
txtstream.WriteLine("    white-Space: nowrap;");
txtstream.WriteLine("}");
```

```
txtstream.WriteLine("div");
txtstream.WriteLine("{");
txtstream.WriteLine("   BORDER-RIGHT: #999999 3px solid;");
txtstream.WriteLine("   PADDING-RIGHT: 6px;");
txtstream.WriteLine("   PADDING-LEFT: 6px;");
txtstream.WriteLine("   FONT-WEIGHT: Normal;");
txtstream.WriteLine("   PADDING-BOTTOM: 6px;");
txtstream.WriteLine("   COLOR: white;");
txtstream.WriteLine("   PADDING-TOP: 6px;");
txtstream.WriteLine("   BORDER-BOTTOM: #999 1px solid;");
txtstream.WriteLine("   BACKGROUND-COLOR: navy;");
txtstream.WriteLine("   FONT-FAMILY: font-family: Cambria, serif;");
txtstream.WriteLine("   FONT-SIZE: 10px;");
txtstream.WriteLine("   text-align: left;");
txtstream.WriteLine("   white-Space: nowrap;");
txtstream.WriteLine("}");
txtstream.WriteLine("span");
txtstream.WriteLine("{");
txtstream.WriteLine("   BORDER-RIGHT: #999999 3px solid;");
txtstream.WriteLine("   PADDING-RIGHT: 3px;");
txtstream.WriteLine("   PADDING-LEFT: 3px;");
txtstream.WriteLine("   FONT-WEIGHT: Normal;");
txtstream.WriteLine("   PADDING-BOTTOM: 3px;");
txtstream.WriteLine("   COLOR: white;");
txtstream.WriteLine("   PADDING-TOP: 3px;");
txtstream.WriteLine("   BORDER-BOTTOM: #999 1px solid;");
txtstream.WriteLine("   BACKGROUND-COLOR: navy;");
```

```
txtstream.WriteLine("    FONT-FAMILY: font-family: Cambria, serif;");
txtstream.WriteLine("    FONT-SIZE: 10px;");
txtstream.WriteLine("    text-align: left;");
txtstream.WriteLine("    white-Space: nowrap;");
txtstream.WriteLine("    display: inline-block;");
txtstream.WriteLine("    width: 100%;");
txtstream.WriteLine("}");
txtstream.WriteLine("textarea");
txtstream.WriteLine("{");
txtstream.WriteLine("    BORDER-RIGHT: #999999 3px solid;");
txtstream.WriteLine("    PADDING-RIGHT: 3px;");
txtstream.WriteLine("    PADDING-LEFT: 3px;");
txtstream.WriteLine("    FONT-WEIGHT: Normal;");
txtstream.WriteLine("    PADDING-BOTTOM: 3px;");
txtstream.WriteLine("    COLOR: white;");
txtstream.WriteLine("    PADDING-TOP: 3px;");
txtstream.WriteLine("    BORDER-BOTTOM: #999 1px solid;");
txtstream.WriteLine("    BACKGROUND-COLOR: navy;");
txtstream.WriteLine("    FONT-FAMILY: font-family: Cambria, serif;");
txtstream.WriteLine("    FONT-SIZE: 10px;");
txtstream.WriteLine("    text-align: left;");
txtstream.WriteLine("    white-Space: nowrap;");
txtstream.WriteLine("    width: 100%;");
txtstream.WriteLine("}");
txtstream.WriteLine("select");
txtstream.WriteLine("{");
txtstream.WriteLine("    BORDER-RIGHT: #999999 3px solid;");
```

```
txtstream.WriteLine("    PADDING-RIGHT: 6px;");
txtstream.WriteLine("    PADDING-LEFT: 6px;");
txtstream.WriteLine("    FONT-WEIGHT: Normal;");
txtstream.WriteLine("    PADDING-BOTTOM: 6px;");
txtstream.WriteLine("    COLOR: white;");
txtstream.WriteLine("    PADDING-TOP: 6px;");
txtstream.WriteLine("    BORDER-BOTTOM: #999 1px solid;");
txtstream.WriteLine("    BACKGROUND-COLOR: navy;");
txtstream.WriteLine("    FONT-FAMILY: font-family: Cambria, serif;");
txtstream.WriteLine("    FONT-SIZE: 10px;");
txtstream.WriteLine("    text-align: left;");
txtstream.WriteLine("    white-Space: nowrap;");
txtstream.WriteLine("    width: 100%;");
txtstream.WriteLine("}");
txtstream.WriteLine("input");
txtstream.WriteLine("{");
txtstream.WriteLine("    BORDER-RIGHT: #999999 3px solid;");
txtstream.WriteLine("    PADDING-RIGHT: 3px;");
txtstream.WriteLine("    PADDING-LEFT: 3px;");
txtstream.WriteLine("    FONT-WEIGHT: Bold;");
txtstream.WriteLine("    PADDING-BOTTOM: 3px;");
txtstream.WriteLine("    COLOR: white;");
txtstream.WriteLine("    PADDING-TOP: 3px;");
txtstream.WriteLine("    BORDER-BOTTOM: #999 1px solid;");
txtstream.WriteLine("    BACKGROUND-COLOR: navy;");
txtstream.WriteLine("    FONT-FAMILY: font-family: Cambria, serif;");
txtstream.WriteLine("    FONT-SIZE: 12px;");
```

```
txtstream.WriteLine("    text-align: left;");

txtstream.WriteLine("    display: table-cell;");

txtstream.WriteLine("    white-Space: nowrap;");

txtstream.WriteLine("    width: 100%;");

txtstream.WriteLine("}");

txtstream.WriteLine("h1 {");

txtstream.WriteLine("color: antiquewhite;");

txtstream.WriteLine("text-shadow: 1px 1px 1px black;");

txtstream.WriteLine("padding: 3px;");

txtstream.WriteLine("text-align: center;");

txtstream.WriteLine("box-shadow: inset 2px 2px 5px rgba(0,0,0,0.5);, inset -2px -2px 5px rgba(255,255,255,0.5);;");

txtstream.WriteLine("}");

txtstream.WriteLine("</style>");
```

www.ingramcontent.com/pod-product-compliance
Lightning Source LLC
Chambersburg PA
CBHW070845070326
40690CB00009B/1709